ESCAPE YOUR **INVISIBLE PRISON:**
9 Secrets for Setting Yourself FREE

Sara,
Thank you! I hope you enjoy the book. It was a pleasure meeting you!

Sam Shver

This book is dedicated to the man whose work saved my life:

John Bradshaw,
Philosopher, Counselor, Theologian and Teacher
1933 - 2016

ESCAPE YOUR INVISIBLE PRISON

9 *Secrets for* **Setting Yourself FREE**

SUSAN ARMSTRONG

ESCAPE YOUR **INVISIBLE PRISON:**
9 Secrets for Setting Yourself FREE

First published in 2017 by
Panoma Press Ltd
48 St Vincent Drive, St Albans, Herts, AL1 5SJ UK

info@panomapress.com
www.panomapress.com

Cover design by Michael Inns
Artwork by Karen Gladwell

ISBN 978-1-784521-09-7

The rights of Susan Armstrong to be identified as the author of this work have been asserted in accordance with sections 77 and 78 of the Copyright, Designs and Patents Act 1988.

A CIP catalogue record for this book is available from the British Library.

All rights reserved. No part of this work may be reproduced in any material form (including photocopying or storing in any medium by electronic means and whether or not transiently or incidentally to some other use of this publication) without the written permission of the copyright holder except in accordance with the provisions of the Copyright, Designs and Patents Act 1988. Applications for the copyright holder's written permission to reproduce any part of this publication should be addressed to the publishers.

This book is available online and in all good bookstores.

Copyright © 2017 Susan Armstrong

Contents

	The Beginning	vii
Part One:	**The Science of the Invisible Prison**	**1**
SECRET #ONE:	The Power of Your Brain	3
SECRET #TWO:	You Are the Centre of Your Own Universe	15
SECRET #THREE:	The Self-Fulfilling Prophecy	25
SECRET #FOUR:	Your Secret Weapon: Confidence and Self-Esteem	35
SECRET #FIVE:	Five Proven Techniques for Developing Self-Esteem	51
SECRET #SIX:	Daily Activities for Developing Self-Esteem	67
Part Two:	**Harness the Power of the Universe and Set Yourself Free**	**87**
SECRET #SEVEN:	The Science of The Universe	89
SECRET #EIGHT:	Universal Truths (Spirituality)	103
SECRET #NINE:	How to Manifest The Life You Desire	123
	As Your Life Continues	141
	Additional Resources	143
	About the Author	145

Acknowledgements

This book would not have been possible without the assistance of several people: my best friend Cynthia Green who has supported me through all my crazy ideas and nomadic tendencies; my sister Sally Melnyk whom I believed to be my biggest critic with this book, and in fact ended up giving me the best gift possible; and Karen Crawley who spent countless hours editing this book and offering her suggestions.

Thank you all, especially my family, who put up with my constant travelling in my quest for self-growth. I could not do it without you.

And to everyone at Panoma Press, thank you for all the hard work.

The Beginning...

Welcome to *Escape Your Invisible Prison...* for most people the title says it all. So I would suggest that, if you are reading this book, there is something you are not happy with about yourself, your life or your circumstances. Or, maybe there's something you want to do... some change you wish to make... some big event that is happening or has happened in your life that you wish to move through gracefully and with ease. Or maybe there is something missing... love, respect, success at work... That's what this book is about: how we get in our own way of happiness, success and fulfillment in life, in love, and in our careers, and I am a master at this!

I am an expert in this topic, and this book has been a long time coming. I'm an expert because I spent the first 30 or so years of my life doing exactly what I write about in this book – keeping myself locked in an invisible prison of my own making, living a life that I thought everyone else wanted me to live, creating my own dramas, my own problems, all the while being unhappy and blaming it on everything else. Then I had to spend the next 20 plus years trying to figure out how to fix it all, and I'm still working on it now. Every day I learn more, more about myself, more about the Universe and how it works, and more about us, as human beings, and how we work. The journey will never end for me, but I'm hoping that, by sharing some of my learning with you, I can speed up your own transformation.

This is not the usual self-help type of book. It's a blend of science, Spirituality, stories, and even some Quantum Physics. I grew up with a scientific way of thinking, not a religious or spiritual one. I grew up only ever believing what I could see, touch and feel, and so, to re-wire my brain and turn my life around, I turned to what I trusted – science. The science of psychology, which then led to neuroscience. I have always needed some sort of proof. I need to know that if things are true, then *why* are they true? Is there science behind this? But there did come a point where science alone wasn't enough. Science couldn't answer all my questions and so I began to study Spirituality – which you can't see, touch, or feel – which eventually led me to Quantum Physics because, well, as I said, I need to know *why*.

In this book I'll share with you some of my learnings, some stories and examples, and some of the science behind why what I'm saying works. There are also some exercises for you that I have used in my own life to re-wire my brain to find the peace, happiness and success that I so desperately wanted – and that I believe we're all entitled to. But first I want to let you know more about why I wrote this book, just so we're clear that this is very much a case-study and not a theoretical book based on what should work, or what other people have tried. The subject of the case-study happens to be me… so let's start there and look at the case, set the context if you will and allow you to possibly draw some parallels with your own life.

I'm happy and successful these days as an International Speaker and Trainer, Author, Wife and Mother, but that hasn't always been the case. I came from a good family: middle-class mother, father, and sister. Both my parents worked to support us and I do not recall wanting for anything growing up, except to be my own person. I am from the UK where I was born and lived as did my parents and their parents before them and so on. And I was raised with (what in my mind I understood to be) two very important beliefs:

1. *If you want other people to like you, you must be perfect (my mother was a perfectionist).*
2. *The greatest sin of all is to hurt someone else's feelings or "put someone out". Other people's feelings are to be looked after at all costs.*

Basically, therefore, I grew up as a people-pleasing perfectionist. Sound familiar? It's not terribly uncommon and I'll refer to these examples throughout this book to demonstrate how these early beliefs got in my way – and, OK, fine, I'll admit it... occasionally still do.

By the time I was 10 years old I couldn't take it anymore. Trying to be all things to all people all the time takes a lot of energy and creates a lot of stress, especially for a child – although I'm guessing you already know this. So, after suffering migraine headaches from the tender age of 7 because of all the stress I put myself under to be perfect, I checked out of the human race at 10 years old. I can still remember the night I sat in bed and said to myself "OK, I'm done. If I can't fit in, if I can't measure up, then I'm going to stop trying". It was shortly after that that I picked up alcohol and drugs. You can probably write the rest of the story yourself because I spent the next 20 years addicted, abused, property of a motorcycle gang and eventually homeless. I had what the police call "no fixed address" from 1977 to 1991. I even wrote a book about my experiences during this period of my life called *An Invisible Prison*. The fact that I lived through all of this, even against the odds, is a miracle and one of the reasons why I have had to accept that not everything can be explained by my beloved science.

After spending 20 years living on the streets, I finally managed to escape. I made it back to the country where my parents were. And while travelling back I had visions of how wonderful it was going to be... how happy and peaceful it would be and how successful I would be! I was running back, back to dreams of balloons at the airport with "Welcome home Sue" written on them, of everyone being happy to see me and of how wonderful life would be. Of course, as I'm sure you've guessed – that's not what happened. Instead of the happy, peaceful, wonderful world I imagined I would come back to, I came back to a world I didn't understand. After being the property of a gang so long – which, let's face it, is really a cult – and so badly addicted and abused, I didn't understand the world anymore. I didn't fit it because of the brainwashing and I couldn't assimilate. And no matter how hard I tried I just couldn't seem to make it work. I was a low-life. Trailer trash. I did not belong with these normal people. I knew it, and I was darned sure they knew it too.

I was so despondent about my life, myself really, that I spent the next year or so actively trying to kill myself. I couldn't look in the mirror without thinking about all the horrible things that had happened in the past, believing it was all my fault. I couldn't see a future… I didn't fit in, and looking in the mirror was a low-life who didn't deserve to be among regular people. Committing suicide with drugs and alcohol seemed to be the only logical thing to do and so I tried… and tried, and tried some more. Thankfully, it didn't work. And I couldn't figure out why… apparently I was such a loser I couldn't even commit suicide! I'm making light of it now, but I remember how horrible I felt at the time. I wanted out of this world. It would be better for me, and better for everyone who knew me – of that I was convinced.

It was a time when I was in such a bad state that I couldn't work anymore. I was too far gone in my addiction. One day I remember lying on my father's couch. My father who so very kindly agreed to take his mess of a daughter back in. He loved me. He was trying to help and he was always my saviour, and so there I lay on the couch… looking at the ceiling… talking to the ceiling: "Why won't you let me die?" I asked. "Why? Please… just let me get hit by a bus while I'm crossing the street. No one will be surprised. No one will care. They'll be relieved… please… just let me die". I didn't know who I was talking to or why, I didn't know why I was still alive even though I had spent 20 years actively trying to destroy myself, I only knew that I was still alive and I wasn't happy with that. I have always been smart, part of the problem I'm sure, and eventually, even through the alcoholic haze, I came to realise that I used to be able to work and I wondered why it was that I couldn't work now – what was different? I decided to try working again, part time, just to start.

Well, it took two shifts at the local bar before I was gone again. This time it was with a man I believed could look after me, and he kind of did. I ended up quitting working in bars and I got a job in a ladies clothing store. AND, more importantly, I quit drinking. At least that's what I told myself. I didn't really. The point was that I only had about four hangovers in one year. For me that was quitting. Things were going fairly well until one day in May. It was a beautiful morning and I didn't have to be at work until noon and I decided that it was such a nice morning I should have a beer. Well, that's pretty much "all she wrote" as they say. The last thing I remember is taking delivery of a case of beer from a taxi driver and calling my boss to tell her that I was a lousy employee, an even worse human being, she shouldn't have hired me in the first place, she deserved a better employee than me, and I quit.

The next thing I knew it was morning. I reached beside my bed, opened a bottle of warm beer, took two swigs, walked over to the sink and dumped the rest of the bottle down the drain. That was the last time I ever touched alcohol or drugs. Why? I don't know. I just knew that if I continued the way I was I would die, and if I didn't continue the way I was I would die. It was time. It was like someone tapped me on the shoulder and said, "OK, enough now". My journey really began that day.

The day I finally decided to give up – because that's what I did, I didn't just give up alcohol, I surrendered – was a miracle which I will share with you later, and that miracle landed me in rehab. When I started to come out of the alcoholic fog and get better, I began to wonder how I had got so bad in the first place. You see, there were no markers. I was a smart child, I had two parents who loved me, a sister. Hell, we even had a white picket fence! There were no alcohol or drug problems in the family, there was no divorce… really no reason for me to go off the rails so badly and at such a young age (I was 11 when I took my first drink). I needed to know why… why had this happened to me?

This set me on a long journey of studying the science of the brain, because that's how I was raised – with a scientific approach. There must be a reason I ended up like this and I was hoping that science would provide it. And while I learned a lot in 10 years studying the science of the brain, it couldn't answer all my questions, so I turned to Spirituality and spent another 10 years studying that to try to understand exactly what had happened to me and how I had ended up this way. By this time, I was wondering "why me?" Why didn't I die when I should have? Logic says that with a life like mine I should have died. I should not be here today doing what I'm doing. And yet, I am. What is my purpose?

After almost 20 years of studying, of applying what I was learning to re-wire my brain, I began to wonder – was it one or the other? Was it science or Spirituality? Which did I believe? I know certain things to be true in psychology... but I also know certain things to be true in Spirituality. So how does that work? This led me to my current field of study: Quantum Physics. Now before you get scared and close the book let me explain... when scientists or physicians write books they are sciency (yes, I know, it's not a word but it is an accurate description). There are long sentences and big words and complex ideas and theories. This is not what this is. This is my interpretation of what I have learned in these past 20 plus years. It is how I understand the science, the Spirituality and the physics and how it fits together for me. It is me sharing how this has worked for me and I have to believe that if it works for me, it can work for you too!

But let me be clear: I am not a physician, physicist, psychologist or philosopher, although my soul is all of these and I have studied these fields for years but not because I wanted a degree in any one discipline. My journey was not a conscious choice but rather a necessity. This has been a very personal journey of discovery for me... discovering how I ended up like I did – homeless, addicted, abused and alone, and of discovering how to re-wire my brain so that I could become a functioning member of society. I didn't learn all of this for any other reason than to apply it. And that's what makes this book different. Yes, I'm going to talk about science and Quantum Physics and Spirituality, but I'm going to explain how they work, and how they work together. I'm going to explain how they worked for me, and show you how they can work for you too.

Because believe me, if you had told me 25 years ago that I would one day be travelling around the world as a Professional Speaker, speaking at conferences, designing and conducting leadership training for the largest companies in the world, and writing books, I would have thought you were crazy. Or at best high on drugs yourself! And yet here I am. This is how we keep ourselves locked in our own invisible prison, we limit ourselves by what we believe is possible, when the truth is that we don't know what is possible for us! Isn't it time you set yourself free?

Here is your first challenge... while reading this book try to put aside your own pre-conceived ideas and notions. Notice when the self-talk starts: "Yes, but...", "Well I can't do that because...", "Well it's not the same because...", "I'm different because..." Stop yourself when you catch yourself saying these things because here's the first secret to releasing yourself from your invisible prison:

You believe you are different. We all believe we are different. Everyone on this planet secretly believes they are different. And it is in this believing that we are different that we are really all the same.

When we engage in the "I'm different because...", "Yes, but...", and every other excuse or reason we come up with for why something doesn't apply to us or won't work, we're taking ourselves out of the game. We are removing ourselves from a possible solution. We are separating ourselves from others by keeping ourselves locked in our invisible prison. We're not separate. We are the same. So rather than focusing on how you are different from others, instead, start noticing how you are the same. Focusing on the differences keeps us separate, it keeps us apart. Focusing on where we are similar (and trust me, the situations may be different but the pain is the same) brings us together.

I am an expert at how we get in our own way, I'm an expert in how we keep ourselves locked in an invisible prison of our own making because I've done it... and occasionally continue to do it today.

This world is a miraculous place if you believe and if you can get out of your own way long enough to let these miracles occur. You will have heard the saying "There is no such thing as a coincidence". Well, there isn't, only a divine plan just for you. So let's get on with it so you can figure out how to free yourself from your invisible prison and live the life you were meant to have.

A Note to the Reader

Before you begin this book, I would like to make you aware that there is repetition: *Repetitio est mater studiorum.* It's Latin for "Repetition is the mother of all learning".

You will find several phrases and concepts repeated in this book, saying the same things over again in a different manner. This is not an accident – it is by design. Repetition is what will help you to create those new neural pathways that will help you to re-program your operating system: thinking is a habit and it takes on average 66 attempts to develop a new habit. Each time I can remind you, or get you to think about these habits or belief systems, you are that much closer to developing new ones.

Some of us can hear or read an idea or concept and immediately understand it. Others (including me) need more of a "2x4" method – meaning we need to be beaten over the head with it several times before it sinks in!

PART ONE:
The Science of the Invisible Prison

"An educated man is not, necessarily, one who has an abundance of general or specialized knowledge. An educated man is one who has so developed the faculties of his mind that he may acquire anything he wants, or its equivalent, without violating the rights of others."

Napoleon Hill, *Think and Grow Rich*

SECRET #ONE:

The Power of Your Brain

"A life without self-examination is one not worth living."
Socrates

There is a great television commercial that shows young children, girls playing dress-up, admiring themselves in mirrors and generally twirling around and being happy in who they are. The commercial asks: "So what happened?" Meaning, we're not born doubting ourselves, being unhappy with ourselves, settling for less than what we deserve. We don't start out being self-conscious, believing we aren't pretty enough, smart enough or good enough. Watch young children. Happy, playful, inquisitive and fearless! They think they are awesome! As did we when we were children, so what happened? How do we end up disliking ourselves so much? How do we end up thinking we aren't good enough, that we don't deserve? We'll explore this idea in this chapter because while we didn't start out this way, we certainly learned to be this way. Now we must unlearn it.

Here's the unfortunate truth: If you are not getting what you want out of life you have only one place to look and that's in the mirror. Everything you can possibly want is there waiting for you, but you have to get out of your own way first. You have to free yourself from the invisible prison of your own making! That's a very strong statement, and I can feel you right now bristling at the suggestion that you somehow have a hand in your own unhappiness or loneliness; that you have played a role if you don't have the job or promotion that you want; or your love life is in a shambles. I can hear what's going on in your mind:

- *"It's not my fault! My boss is an idiot... he refuses to see all the great work I do!"*
- *"It's not my fault... my co-worker always does this! I do the work, she takes the credit!"*
- *"It's not my fault... I've tried to find love. Men/women are idiots. There are no good men/women out there."*
- *"I attract losers."*
- *"Nothing good ever happens to me..."*
- *"It's not my fault I'm unhappy... if my husband/wife/children/boss/co-workers/friends would only.... (insert whatever you wish) then I'd be happy!"*
- *"I'm miserable, I don't know how my life turned out this way..."*
- *"People are not to be trusted... everyone lets you down."*
- *"It's just the way life is. You have to grin and bear it!"*
- *"It's not my fault... this is the way I am... I can't change..."*
- *"Yes, but..."*

Well, I'm sorry but it's true. We get in the way of our own success. Whatever is happening within you, whatever is happening in your life right now that you are unhappy with, you had a hand in creating.

I'll say it again: Whatever is happening within you, whatever is happening in your life right now that you are unhappy with, you had a hand in creating.

We all have choices, and it is your choices throughout your life that have led you to this point. Good or bad, you have created your existence. No one else. You don't have to like this, but you have to accept this. It doesn't matter what happens outside of you, it only matters what happens inside of you and here is where the big problem lies. The good news is, it stands to reason, if you created it, you can UN-create it... or create something different! Aristotle said: "We are what we repeatedly do. Excellence, then, is not an act, but a habit." If we continue to do the same things we've always done, we will get what we've always got. If we wish our lives to change then we need to change, we need to do something differently: think differently, change our beliefs, change our attitudes, and/or change our actions.

I know this, because I am a master at standing in my own way, at keeping myself locked in an invisible prison that I create in my own mind. I am an expert in how to sabotage oneself. I didn't set out to do that, but that's what happened. In part, I believe it happened because of the way I was raised… believing that I had to be perfect for people to like me, believing that I had to make people happy all the time. I was probably only about two or three years old when I got the message that nothing I did was ever going to be good enough for my mother. This "not good enough", this sense of "not being worthy" was imprinted in my subconscious a long time ago, before I was even aware of it. And, in my mind, since I wasn't good enough for my mother, who gave birth to me, then how could I ever be good enough for anyone else? These subconscious thoughts drove my thoughts, feelings, actions and behaviours for many, many years, and they still pop up occasionally, even now.

In Western societies, we place a great deal of emphasis on our ability to think, to be rational, and to make good decisions through analysis, and to process information and problem solve. And these are great abilities housed in the neo-cortex, the thinking part of our brain. The problem is that in my experience these cognitive or conscious abilities are not our power source and I want to point out that there is science to back me up. I spent years studying the brain and why we do what we do to try to understand how I ended up the way I did, and this is my non-technical way of explaining what I learned.

The Source of Your Power

Our power source lies in our unconscious mind. It's our unconscious mind that drives us a lot of the time, it causes us to act and react in certain ways, and it was programmed a long time ago. Logic has nothing to do with it. Let's go back to the example of young children.

We are not born with the logical, rational part of our brain functioning. It develops as we grow. When we are born, we do not have the ability to reason, to rationalise, to make decisions. Have you ever heard yourself saying to your child: "Don't do that! It's dangerous! What were you thinking?" Well, the simple answer is, they weren't thinking because they do not have the thinking or reasoning ability of an adult. It has not yet developed. A two-year-old does not understand what a "hot stove" is… that is until they touch it. They are new to this world and have no frame of reference. As infants and children, we process things through our emotional centre.

This is an important piece of information to know because as children, from the time we are born we communicate – we send and receive messages through non-verbal means: emotions, body language, touch, facial expression, tone of voice, inflection, pitch, pace, and volume. (There is some evidence to support the notion that babies respond to their mother's voice while still in the womb.) Young children do not yet understand words, and even if they did, they do not have the ability to process them. Even when they are old enough to understand words, they do not have the ability to process them for correct meaning.

To a child, their parents or primary caregivers are the be-all and end-all. They are the most important role models in a child's early life. As children, we learn from our primary caregivers, we learn what is modelled for us. For a child, when a parent says something is good or bad, right or wrong, we believe them (keep in mind we have no way of knowing anything else). Children also learn what they have to do to get what they want from their caregivers – love, attention and approval. We learn how to behave, what makes them smile, what makes them angry, and we learn all of this before we can even talk. We learn what "masks" we need to wear to get what we want at a very early age. We learn what love looks like, what relationships look like, how to engage in conflict, how to express feelings… I could go on and on… we learn it all while we are children watching our adult role-models. A favourite quote of mine from Abraham Maslow says:

> *"Every act or thought, every one without exception, records itself in our unconscious and makes us despise or love ourselves more."*

It was suggested to me by a PhD friend that 50% of our emotional programming is set by the time we are three years old, and 80% set by the time we are 18 because of how we are wired as human beings and the very complex way our brain functions. I don't know if this is true, but I have read several articles that would suggest the same thing.

We learned our **conditioned** responses long ago. Long before our thinking, rational brain fully developed we learned about ourselves, about love, about life and about what's possible for us. And we carry that with us throughout our life operating on the belief that it's true. I call this "Centre of the Universe" a condition of being human and we'll explore the power this has on our lives in the next chapter.

For now, what I really want you to understand is the power of this "conditioning", so I'm going to explain a little brain science so you can better understand when I say WE stand in our own way, WE keep ourselves locked in an invisible prison – it's our thinking, our beliefs, our ideas of what is possible that often get in the way of our happiness and success. We don't mean to do this, we don't know we're doing it… it's the power of conditioning, of conditioned responses, of thought and behaviour patterns that we learned a long time ago… long before we were able to really think about, or rationalise, any of it.

The Science of The Brain

The Limbic system or emotional brain is where our emotions reside, where memory begins and where these two functions combine to mark behaviours with positive or negative feelings. It's where mostly unconscious value judgments are made. Information going through the Limbic system is filed under agreeable or disagreeable and it also plays a role in what grabs your attention, spontaneity and creativity. So, if you will bear with me for a minute, here is a simple way of understanding the power of this:

There are many functions housed in the Limbic system controlled by:

THE AMYGDALA – about the size of an almond, it helps in storing and classifying emotionally charged memories. It plays a large role in producing emotions, especially fear.

THE HIPPOCAMPUS – is all about memory and a little about learning. Its primary function is memory formation and classification and long term memory. Like the RAM in your computer, it processes and stores new and temporary memory for long-term storage.

THE HYPOTHALAMUS – is linked closely to the pituitary gland which controls many of the body's functions. It monitors and controls your circadian rhythms, homeostasis – making sure your body is running smoothly – appetite, thirst, other bodily urges, and plays a role in emotions.

THE THALAMUS – is *THE* relay station in the brain. Most of the sensory signals – auditory, visual, somatosensory (skin and internal organs) – go through the Thalamus on their way to other parts of the brain for processing. It also plays a part in motor control.

What's fascinating about this is we tend to believe our thinking and reasoning processes are in control – in fact they are not, they are secondary to our emotional brain.

Even more fascinating to me is how this works: we experience an intense emotion as a child, be it fear, joy, disappointment, whatever it is; this then gets stored in our memory because of the intensity of the emotion and then every time we come across a similar situation or event we respond from our subconscious as if it's the first time it's happened. The problem is that a lot of the time this event/circumstance/situation was imprinted on our subconscious long before we had the ability to think about it logically or rationally and yet we carry these feeling-behaviour combinations through our entire lives. This is the importance of our early childhood experiences. They will often unconsciously drive our emotions and reactions today. The good news is that because they were learned, they can be unlearned. And this is what it's about… bringing the unconscious to the conscious.

We often fear situations that are not dangerous, like speaking in public. This may come from something as simple as giving a presentation in school, making a mistake and having the class laugh at you. It happened once, and yet it was so emotionally powerful that it imprinted on our subconscious and every time we give a presentation as an adult the subconscious fear raises its head. We are afraid the class will laugh – but we're adults now, we have the power to change that, and the truth is, you don't know if people will laugh or not, you don't know that you'll make a mistake, you don't know anything about what will happen, but since we only have the past to refer to, we go back to that one time... You see the problem?

The Power of Conditioning

Here's a silly example of how the power of conditioning works, and don't worry, I have a million of them! I have spent most of my life afraid of men in blue uniforms. Which is funny when you think about the fact that my husband was a career police officer! Why am I afraid of men in blue uniforms? Because when I was a child my mother used to tell me that if I didn't behave the man in the blue uniform would come and arrest me and take me away. I was a child, I didn't understand that wouldn't happen. I believed my mother and I was afraid and I carried that fear through my life. It was so bad that I was unable to speak coherently with customs officials, I was afraid of fire-fighters, ambulance drivers… anyone wearing a blue uniform. If I was driving down the street and saw a police car anywhere near me I would start to shake and sweat because I was so afraid. And for no reason except for this subconscious fear that was imprinted long ago. So when I discovered this, I brought it to my conscious mind and understood it for what it was – my mother trying to make me behave using whatever means necessary – and I'm glad to say that while it's not completely gone, it does not get in my way anymore.

This is the power of conditioning. It plays an enormous part in who we are and how we live our lives. When we are young our role models teach us what is right and wrong and we have no choice but to believe them. When we are young we can't help but take on the attitudes and beliefs of the people we spend time with. The problem is that what if their beliefs were wrong for us? We take these things as truth when in fact they were only true for that person in that moment. And sometimes it's these beliefs that keep us stuck.

Another example: I was raised to believe that "people like us" don't have their own businesses. I have no idea what that means but it wasn't until my father passed away that I realised how silly that was and I found the courage to start my business. I was raised to believe that when you get in a relationship it's for life – you stay in that relationship whether you like the person or not. Following that belief caused me to stay in some very co-dependant and abusive relationships until I discovered what I was doing and could think about it logically and rationally.

We learn what we live and we live what we learn. The power of conditioning in our lives. And for a lot of us it's an unconscious thing. Think about it – what was your "conditioning"? What beliefs were you raised with? Are you aware of them?

When I was in rehab I became acutely aware of my subconscious belief that I had to be perfect or people wouldn't like me. I want to point out that no one else had to be perfect, just me. Which is ridiculous when you think about it. I also became aware of people-pleasing… the not liking to "put people out" which meant never saying no, never disagreeing, never asking for what I wanted or needed. Again, this was not healthy. I knew I had to work on these things. But this wasn't the worst of it for me, no, it was just the tip of the iceberg. I didn't truly become aware of the power of conditioning in my life until I was over four years sober.

The Event That Changed Everything

Three months before the fifth anniversary of my sobriety, my father was diagnosed with colon cancer. It was eight days from the diagnosis until he died. Eight days. I was devastated. My father and I had always been, and still were, very close. He was my hero, he was my saviour. He was the one that sent me the airline ticket to escape the gang, he let me move in with him, and as long as my father was alive I knew I would always be OK because he would rescue me.

And then he died.

Of all the horrible things that have happened in my life my father dying was by far the worst. I remember driving down the street a day or so after he died and thinking to myself "What's the point? There is no point in living anymore" and I began to once again contemplate suicide. Very quickly those thoughts were replaced by another thought: "NO! That's not how you honour your father's life". And it was in that moment that I truly understood the power of conditioning.

Being of very traditionalist parents I had been raised (or conditioned, if you will) to believe that when you got a job, you stayed at that job until you retired. When you married, you stayed married until you died whether you liked the person or not. And now, here, in my car, contemplating suicide I was confronted with the knowledge that everything I had done in my life was to make my father proud. I had stayed at horrible jobs to make him proud. I had stayed in abusive relationships to make him proud. Everything I had done, including get sober, was to make my father proud. And now he was gone and there was no more reason to do anything.

Now, I had to decide: did I want to continue... knowing, this time I would be doing it for me? It wasn't until my father's death that I understood how truly imprisoned I had been by my conditioning. In my father's death I found freedom for the first time in my life and I can't describe how it felt to be truly free. I hope this doesn't sound horrible... I loved my father dearly, but the power of his influence over me was very strong. And now it was gone and I was free to do whatever I wanted with my life. I had no one to "make proud" anymore. It was a turning point and it was right after my father's death that I started my own business.

Here's the thing – our parents, our primary caregivers, those others we have contact with during the early part of our lives whether it's siblings, friends or family, all contribute to our conditioning, or programming. We don't know whether what they are telling us is right or wrong, as children we don't have the capacity to reason, to think, to make rational decisions. We just believe those we trust. I'll repeat the Abraham Maslow quote one more time:

> "Every act or thought, every one without exception, records itself in our unconscious and makes us despise or love ourselves more."

Our brains, for the most part have been programmed by people outside of ourselves to believe, to think, to feel and behave in certain ways. And then we live our lives based on this early conditioning. Our parents or primary caregivers are our role-models. We learn what we live and then live what we learn. But what if what we learned in those early years isn't true? What if, like my Police Officer example, our role models were wrong?

Our parents do the best they can for us, they do what they believe is right. The problem is that what they are doing, the messages they are imprinting, are right in their world, in their Centre of the Universe, but they may not be right for us. I loved my mother and father. They did the very best they could... they gave me and my sister everything they believed we needed. Please notice I say everything **they** believed we needed. The problem was (and still is) that the messages I grew up with, while right and true for them in their generation and circumstances, were not right for me.

My conditioning caused me no end of discomfort and pain and, literally, drove me to choose drinking to escape the pain. I couldn't be perfect. I couldn't make everyone happy all the time. So rather than be a disappointment to my parents I escaped reality through alcohol and substance abuse. And worse, it took my father dying for me to understand this phenomenon and begin to undo my early programming.

I believed everything I learned... that "people like us" don't become managers, don't own their own businesses, don't go to university... and on and on. The problem for me was that as I grew up, all that conditioning was in direct contradiction to who I was becoming and what I wanted, and the internal conflict between who I was and what I wanted and what my parents thought was the right thing for me was more than I could bear. If you've read my book *An Invisible Prison*, then you know what that internal conflict drove me to – 20 years of self-abuse and abuse at the hands of others, 20 years of trying to actively destroy myself. Why? Because I thought there was something wrong with me. I felt like I was different, that I didn't belong. Well I was different – different from my parents, different from my sister, different from the rest of my family. But that wasn't wrong... different isn't wrong, it's just different, only as a child I didn't know that.

This conditioning, these habitual thinking patterns, can be changed. The habit of how we think creates neural pathways in our brain, meaning that whenever a circumstance presents itself, the thought automatically occurs. But we can change this. We can begin to create new neural pathways, new thought habits, and that's what this book is about. That's how you re-wire your brain! Thought by thought, habit by habit. And no, it's not quick, but with every single change you make you will see a positive result!

If you're still skeptical about the power of this, I assure you, there is plenty of science to back this up. This is all about what I call "the condition of being human", it's about our brain and how we develop and it starts in childhood, and this is my very simplistic way of explaining a very complex topic. If you would like more information, I would recommend going to the internet and researching any one of a multitude of topics around this subject… but be prepared – you could get lost for days in the theories and opinions of different "experts".

How We Keep Ourselves Locked in our Own Invisible Prison

We keep ourselves locked in the invisible prison by living a life based on an operating manual that was imprinted in us when we were children. Someone else's operating manual. Some of which may be right for you – my parents imprinted many things which have been incredibly helpful in my life like my sense of right and wrong. They taught me about unconditional love, they imprinted an incredibly valuable work ethic. I could go on with all the positives, but they imprinted many things which have not been helpful, and not only did these things prevent me from being happy and successful, they caused me a great deal of pain.

We limit ourselves based on (what we believe are) our own ideas, opinions, experience, or worse, others' ideas, opinions and suggestions of what our lives should be. We live our lives and limit ourselves based on "what if's…". Think about it. It happens all the time and I'm sure it's happened to you!

Why are you doing the job you are doing? Is it because you wanted this job? Or is it because you thought it was the only job you could get? Or maybe you're doing this job because your parents thought it was a good job for you?

If you're unhappy in this job, why do you stay? (And by the way, "Because I don't have a choice" is not a reasonable answer but another way we keep ourselves locked in our prison. We *always* have choices).

What about your relationships? Are you happy? If you're not, why do you stay? Are you afraid that you will never find anyone else? Are you afraid that you're too old? Too big/small/not enough/not a nice enough person? Are you afraid you're not good enough, or lovable enough and so you just stay with what you have because it's better than the heartache of trying to go after something different?

And here's the biggest question of all: how do you know that any of these reasons you tell yourself for why you do what you do are even true?

Here's the truth: you don't know what's possible in this world! You only know what you believe is possible based on your experiences, knowledge and information (most of which comes from your conditioning) and you proceed based on that. Doing this seriously limits your prospects! You can do anything you want, have anything you want – you just first have to believe it's possible. Seeing isn't always believing. Sometimes you have to believe to see. So let's work on updating your operating manual!

Begin with this:

- *What is your conditioning? What rules and beliefs do you live by?*
- *What are your earliest memories about right and wrong? What was life like in your house when you were growing up? Can you identify some of your conditioning?*
- *Which of these beliefs or rules need to be looked at and updated for who you are today?*

SECRET #TWO:

You Are the Centre of Your Own Universe

"Human beings can alter their lives by altering their attitudes of mind."
William James

We each believe we are the centre of the universe.

This was one of my most important learnings while trying to re-wire my own brain and overcome all the self-limiting beliefs and behaviours I had accumulated over the years. This learning served, and still serves, as the foundation for all of my growth. I call it a condition of being human. Not right or wrong but rather the science of how our brains are wired. We are born this way. We are born with the "Centre of the Universe" phenomenon.

Basically, the theory is that we, as people, believe we are the centre of the universe and the world revolves around us. Think about it: every thought that goes through your head has something to do with you! How you feel about things, the way you see things, what you want, what you like, what you don't like… when was the last time you had a dream and you weren't in it? We occupy our minds 24 hours a day. Think about this: have you ever followed someone into a store only to see them stop as soon as they go through the door. There they are, stopped, right inside the doorway so no one else can get in or pass, as if they were the only one in the world, completely oblivious to anyone behind them. Or, have you ever walked down a street and there are three or four people ahead of you, chatting together, taking up the entire pavement, completely oblivious to the fact that there are other people who are also on that street and may want to pass?

This is the "Centre of the Universe" phenomenon that we all have. AND, we see it in action every day. Those of you who have children know that young children really, truly believe that the world revolves around them. This is the problem with divorce when children are young. The child can't help but think it's their fault. If a parent becomes ill, the child secretly believes somewhere deep inside they have caused this. It's not right or wrong, good or bad, and we can't change it. It is just the way it is. This is the power of the Centre of the Universe.

I'm sure we've all heard the saying "perception is reality"? This Centre of the Universe phenomenon is the reason that saying is true. As we have discussed in the previous chapter, it is our own unique experiences in life including our conditioning that create filters which govern how we view the world. How old are you? Where are you from? Where have you lived? Who were your parents? Did you have brothers and/or sisters? How many? Did you share a room or have your own? Where did you go to school... and on and on. Everything that has ever happened to you creates these filters, this view of the world. Everything anyone has ever said to you or done to you helps to shape your view of the world. Think about it: how many of you have brothers and sisters who grew up in the same house as you with the same parents and yet you look at them today, shake your head and think "Are you sure we're related?" because they have such a different view of the world than you do? If this can happen in a family, what does this say about the people we come in contact with every day?

We experience everything in relation to ourselves and it's this centre of the universe view that sets the foundation for a lot of our challenges. If we see things one way and others see them a different way then conflict often ensues. It especially gets in our way when it comes to how we should proceed in the world, the difference in right and wrong, in our confidence and self-esteem and even in our belief of what is possible, because however we see things, we assume everyone else sees them the same way. But what did we just say about our upbringing? That we learn right and wrong, how to behave, how to think, our values, our view or perception of the world from our upbringing and experiences in life. So, unless we all had the same parents and exactly the same experiences when growing up then we can't possibly see things the same way. You see? This is the problem. We have a very subjective view of reality.

As we are, so we expect other people to be. The problem is, they aren't like us, we are all unique in our way of viewing the world and, as such, none of us can truly understand how another person views the world. We can get close, but there will still be filters operating that we don't understand.

People-Pleasing

Here's how this issue of conditioning, or our early experiences, contributes to who we are and how we feel and behave today. Before I understood all of this about how our view of the world is formed and this issue of Centre of the Universe, I was always careful to choose my actions and words based on what other people would think; in other words, I did people's thinking for them. I did this because I was raised to believe that you shouldn't inconvenience anyone else or "put them out" (which means ask them to go out of their way to help you). The simplest example of this that I can think of is probably the most common (but stay with me here because this gets very convoluted, a perfect example of what I meant when I said it takes a lot of energy to live life this way):

I would never ask someone to help me do something because in my mind I wouldn't want to do it – so I assumed they wouldn't want to do it either. So rather than asking them for a favour and making them uncomfortable because they would want to say no but they would probably say yes so they didn't hurt my feelings, I would just not ask because then I was doing them a favour. Why? Because in my Centre of the Universe that's what I would do.

Whew. No wonder I was crazy. As I write this now I can clearly remember that feeling of always being on edge, wondering if what I was saying and doing was the right thing. I realised that this was not logical. I had learned this from my mother. She never – and still doesn't – like to "put people out". But that was, and is, her issue, not mine, and this idea of trying to make all people happy all of the time had made me crazy! So I decided I was no longer going to do other people's thinking for them. I was going to stop projecting my Centre of the Universe view onto them. Not my job anymore. Now I only worry about if it's the right thing for me. If I need something I ask for it. How the other person responds is totally up to them.

Centre of the Universe means that people do things they want to do because they want to do them. People do things for reasons that make sense to them. We all get a payoff from whatever activity or behaviour it is we are engaging in. For example, someone who engages in gossip about another person is often doing so to feel better about themselves. All the wonderful souls who spend their spare time in soup kitchens do so because helping others makes them happy as well as having the added benefit of making others happy. I speak at conferences and do workshops because being able to pass along my knowledge and help others find happiness makes me feel good. Each person's behaviour is up to that individual. All people make choices based on what they believe will bring them peace and/or happiness and/or love. We all have choices and we can behave any way we choose. Therefore, I really didn't have the power to force anyone to do anything, or control the things they were already doing. It was all an illusion! Huh! Who knew? Certainly not me! But this is the power of Centre of the Universe thinking and it operates in all of us.

The truth about human beings is we all believe we are the centre of the universe, we are all driven by our filters and perceptions, but what you must know is that because of this fact, we often stand in our own way. We keep ourselves locked in the invisible prison in our mind because we operate on self-limiting beliefs as a result of our childhood or conditioning. We operate on our own beliefs about life, relationships, happiness, what's possible, and what life should or shouldn't be. But these are just that: *OUR* beliefs based on *OUR* filters or *OUR* view of the world! And none of this may actually be true out there in reality!

Our perception is our reality. Before I understood this Centre of the Universe phenomenon, I had always assumed that everyone saw things and believed the same way I did. Which meant, because I felt like I didn't fit in, because I wasn't perfect, because I didn't believe I could do anything right, because I believed I was worthless... I believed that everyone else thought the same thing about me. This is the problem with our Centre of the Universe – we project our beliefs, thoughts, opinions and ideas onto everyone else.

So, if I think I'm worthless, I automatically assume everyone else thinks I'm worthless as well. And what does this mean? It means that because of the way our brains are wired and the power of filters, I will only pay attention to things that support my view of the world. Anything that conflicts with my view or beliefs I think is wrong.

I'm hoping by now you see the problem with this! **The problem with this is that because of Centre of the Universe none of this is true out there in reality!** It is only my subjective view, from my Centre of the Universe.

But I didn't know this. And because it was my view, and I believed that made it a fact, I acted on it. For me that showed up in different ways: I hid, I pretended I wasn't smart, I didn't speak up, I wouldn't look people in the eye, I dressed in ways that supported my view of being worthless... why? Because I was afraid that if people noticed me they would... what I don't know, but something devastating would happen. They would realise how worthless I was and kick me off the planet... or I would turn to dust and blow away. I'm not sure what I thought would happen, only that it would be devastating. My Centre of the Universe... my knowing I wasn't good enough (because of my perfectionistic upbringing), my knowing I was different... I hung this on others and automatically assumed they saw me the same way and believed the same thing about me.

It's Not About You... It Never Is

Here's something else I didn't know: because of our Centre of the Universe orientation I thought all eyes were on me all the time. Noticing everything I did wrong, everything I said wrong, seeing all the reasons I didn't belong just like I did. But that's not the case. Because of Centre of the Universe no one was paying attention to me... they were busy thinking about themselves – how they felt, what was wrong in their lives, how unhappy they were. And if they were looking at me it was only in comparison to themselves.

This is what we fail to recognise... that everyone is too busy worrying about themselves and their situation to notice ours, and yet we walk around convinced there is a flashing red LED sign on our forehead that says "worthless". OK, maybe not all of us, but I certainly did. Maybe yours says something else: "damaged", "horrible human being", "loser", don't deserve to be here", "not lovable", "not good enough". Whatever it is, we are convinced it's on display for the world to see! But it's not! It only resides in your mind! It's your perception, your truth – not anyone else's. And when we act on this truth we create self-fulfilling prophecies (which is covered in the next chapter) and that's one of the ways we stand in our own way.

So let's turn this around. In the next chapter, we'll look at how our Centre of the Universe creates self-fulfilling prophecies. Some of them are good, some of them bad. For now, what you need to know is that whatever anyone else says or does has more to do with them than it does with you!! It's not about you! If someone says to you, "I don't like that blouse", what do you do? If you don't believe you are good enough, or worthy enough, then you believe what they say is true because it supports your beliefs about yourself. But really, what they are saying is, "In my view of the world that blouse is not very nice". In *their view of the world*. It has nothing to do with you! They are sharing with you *THEIR* Centre of the Universe which is different from yours. So, don't take it personally. Whatever anyone says or does is telling you something about them... it has nothing to do with you!! No one has the power to make anyone else happy, angry, sad, frustrated, or anything else. No one else is in charge of your brain, your feelings, your thoughts and behaviours. Only you are! So again I say… if there is something that is not working in your life you have only to go to the closest mirror to find the solution.

Everyone is the Centre of their own Universe. This isn't a switch we can turn off or on. It is present and operating in all of us all the time. We have to stop worrying about what other people think – that's on them. They are comparing or measuring things to their view of the world – which is fine. You just can't take it on as your own reality. You can't take it on as truth. It's an opinion. And we're all entitled to them.

Which brings me to the issue of families and conditioning from the last chapter. Your parents did what they thought was right for you. They did the best they could with the skills and knowledge they had. They did the best they could according to their Centre of the Universe, their subjective view of what was right and possible. This doesn't mean that everything you were taught, everything you believe, all the unwritten rules, are necessarily correct. Take for example my own conditioning, my own unwritten rules that in order for people to like you, you must be perfect. That you shouldn't upset someone else and saying "no" was upsetting, so you should always be all things to all people all the time.

Still to this day my Mother (bless her) tries to force her ideas of right and wrong on to me. She still says things like "Why do you do this? When are you going to stop? Why can't you just settle down?" Because I travel, because I move houses on a regular basis, because I like 'different', I like change, I love a good challenge. And she doesn't understand. In her view of the world people should be settled, they should be stable and secure, they should know what to expect. And I do not believe such things. I believe that life is to be lived! Life is meant for us to have as many experiences as possible, and the ultimate goal in life is to live up to one's full potential. I'm a risk taker. Not the way I was raised, but what I learned to become after my father passed away. And that is not in keeping with my mother's view of the world. So, we have conflict.

Who are You Living Your Life For?

And this is the point, at least for me – you have to make your own choice: whose life is it anyway? What do you want for your life? Do you want to live your life to make your parents (or someone else) proud? Or do you want to live your life to make yourself proud?

Your parents, family, friends, co-workers don't have to approve of your choices. Sure, it's nice if they do… but you can't live your life for them. You must live it for you! Your happiness is your job, your business. No one else can make you happy, only you can. So, what does that look like for you?

I can't even tell you how many clients I have who are miserable, de-motivated, just going through the motions in life, like they are sleepwalking and just trying to get to death safely. Why? Because they are living a life that is not what they want but one that was created for them or was expected of them. This is not happiness, peace and success. This is being trapped in an invisible prison!

We can't help but project our past experiences onto present or future circumstances. After all, what is in our mind, what is in our past experience, is all we have to refer to. But when we hang our expectations on others, we will always be disappointed. And this is part of the problem. We have a very limited view – of ourselves, of others and what they think, feel, and believe, and a very limited view of what is possible in this life. Some of us are more limited than others.

I've said it before – we need to update our operating manual!

Here's the thing: all of us really only want one thing – to feel important, and this is true throughout our entire lives. When we are young we learn to behave in certain ways, to say and do certain things to gain the approval of those around us, to feel loved and valued. We learn to wear masks. The problem is that we are not aware we are doing it, or why we are doing it, we just feel we have to. And we continue throughout our lives wearing those same masks, trying to get what we want and then wondering why it's not working. It's time to take the masks off and see reality for what it is.

In the first chapter I gave you some scientific information about how our brain forms and operates to explain how some of these thoughts, feelings, behaviours, unwritten rules we live by and view of the world happen to us, how they get imprinted on us. In this chapter we've focused on how our view of the world gets projected onto people, places and things and how we respond to that projected reality as if it's the truth. This is really important. If we truly desire to re-wire our brain, to escape our invisible prison, then we must work on uncovering the beliefs, thoughts, unwritten rules and view of the world that are guiding us. We must step back and ask: is this true? Is this relevant for me now? Is this helping me or hurting me? Here are some thoughts to get you started...

- *As you go through your day today, begin to notice this "Centre of the Universe" phenomenon. Notice how many people behave as if they are the only ones in the world. There is plenty of evidence out there if you look for it.*

- *Start to notice your thoughts, reactions and feelings – notice how quick you are to jump to it being about you. When someone fails to hold a door open for you – what do you think? When someone makes a comment to you – do you take it personally?*

- *Start to notice how you make everything about you (keeping in mind this is not bad or good, but rather a condition of being human). How many times do you say "I" in a day?*

- *Start to notice where other people have different opinions or ideas... how do you respond? Do you take it personally because they don't agree with you?*

- *Ask yourself: is it possible that your view of the world might not be the only one? Is it possible that your view of yourself and your life might be just that? YOUR view? Might other people believe or feel a different way about you? (We'll work more on this one in the Confidence Chapter.*

SECRET #THREE:

The Self-Fulfilling Prophecy

"If you think you can do a thing, or think you can't do a thing, you're right."
Henry Ford

Ah... the outcome of both our conditioning and our Centre of the Universe orientation – the self-fulfilling prophecy. Meaning: whatever we put out there is what we will get back!

Let's review where we're at: we take on the beliefs, ideas and opinions of those closest to us while we're growing up. It's impossible not to. And we believe them. We believe our parents' idea of what is right and what is wrong and we believe that since we are the centre of the universe and we see things a certain way, others must see things the same way. In fact, nothing could be further from the truth. Your unique view of yourself and the world around you is just that, your unique view. And whatever you put out there is what you will get back. Meaning, we create or attract our own situation or circumstances based on our view of ourselves and our world. We create a self-fulfilling prophecy. We create what we believe.

I have said that if things are not going right in your life you need look no further than the nearest mirror for the cause. This is the secret – this is why self-esteem and confidence are so important, and why there is more than one chapter in this book on developing confidence and self-esteem. The more highly you value yourself, the better your life will become because you will attract and create what you believe you are worth. Therefore, confidence and self-esteem are your power base.

The Self-Fulfilling Prophecy

Here's how the self-fulfilling prophecy works, and it happens in each moment, with each thought, in each situation: your thoughts and beliefs about yourself, about situations and circumstances, about other people (your self-esteem) drive your expectations (I can't do it, I'm worthless).

In turn, your expectations influence your behaviour, which creates the outcome. The outcome confirms your belief and expectation and so it perpetuates the cycle. It's why the Henry Ford quote is so true: *"If you think you can do a thing, or you think you can't do a thing, you're right."* You can go to my Facebook Page @eyipuk and watch a video that explains this cycle.

This self-fulfilling prophecy happens all the time in our lives but I need to get a little sciency to explain it. We always think of communication as being words but it's so much more than that. According to a widely-quoted study done by Professor Albert Mehrabian, when it comes to communication, only 7% of our meaning comes from the words we use, 38% of the meaning comes from how we say those words and 55% of our communication comes from our body language and facial expressions while we are saying the words. Studies continue to be done on communication and how it happens, and while scientists disagree on the actual statistics, what is agreed on is that it's not so much the words that communicate but the energy behind the words that comes out through our tone of voice and inflection, our body language, and the energy or vibration that we are putting out into the Universe.

Like attracts like. Your view of the world, your view of yourself, of other people, of situations, of what is possible in this life – your Centre of the Universe if you will – is called your "attitude". Attitude according to the dictionary is a "position indicating a particular mental state". In other words, how you feel about people, places and things. Well, like it or not you are wearing your attitude all the time. You are telling people your attitude about yourself, your life, your job, the world, about them, all the time through your body language and voice tone and inflection.

If you recall from the first chapter – the science of all of this –it is not your reasoning, logical Neo-Cortex that is in control of your brain, it's your Limbic system. Words come from your logical, thinking brain. Body language, voice tone and inflection, your energy, come from your emotional brain. What that means is that words can lie, but your energy, your body language, your voice tone and inflection can't and that's why you are always wearing your attitude.

Back to the self-fulfilling prophecy. If I think I'm worthless (which I did for many years) then what is my expectation of others? That they think I'm worthless too. And what does that do to my behaviour? It might cause me to people-please, to avoid people, to not make friends or socialise, to accept people treating me in less than respectful ways. Why? Because that's what I believe and expect. And when they do these things, and I accept it (because it's all I deserve), then I say: "See... I knew it... I'm worthless!" and I get the exact outcome I expected!

How We Create a Self-Fulfilling Prophecy

I perpetuated this cycle throughout my life. I can remember feeling so worthless that I would question whether or not I would get a job and because my expectations of myself were so low I would go to the lowest job and apply for that. Of course, I would get the job (I'm actually quite smart and talented – I was the only one that didn't know it), and then I would say to myself "See, this horrible job – it's the only one I could get" and I would use it as proof of my worthlessness.

Or my favourite... when I was so convinced that I wouldn't get the job that I didn't even show up to the interview on time! Of course I didn't get the job, and then used that as further proof to myself of my worthlessness. Oh my... the things we do to ourselves. Unfortunately, our brains will always find evidence to prove our beliefs correct and so we end up creating the very thing we believe will happen and we get the outcome we expected and it perpetuates the cycle.

Here's another example of how we create these self-fulfilling prophecies: I want to ask for a raise but I don't believe my boss will say yes. When I finally summon up the courage to go in and ask, I stutter and stammer, say "uhm" a lot, look at the floor instead of her/him… basically come across as not very confident in my request because I'm afraid she/he's going to say no, and what happens? I don't get the raise. There is no surprise there. If I'm not confident, if I don't believe I deserve a raise why should my boss?

Or, if you get really nervous before you have to speak in public or at a meeting, then you probably have a less than positive view of your effectiveness in such situations. But it's really not the nervousness that's important – it's how we perceive it. Everyone gets nervous before speaking in public – I've been a Professional Speaker for 20 years and I still get nervous! If you get nervous before you speak, if you think you are going to make a mistake or say something wrong, if you believe that you don't know enough about the topic or can't answer questions, if you are afraid you are going to fail… then you will fail. If you get nervous before speaking to your boss or your colleague whom you find intimidating, or a senior manager, if you worry that you'll make a fool of yourself and the words won't come out, then, likely, you will freeze and look silly in front of this person.

Creating a Positive Self-Fulfilling Prophecy

This is why we need to create positive prophecies instead of negative ones, and the good news is that you can break the cycle, you can turn it into a positive instead of a negative. Your thoughts and beliefs, this conditioning, your opinion of yourself, who you are, what you believe you deserve in this life are powerful. You will attract and create or allow whatever you believe. This was a powerful learning for me. I realised that I had a thinking problem – it was my thoughts, my beliefs, my feelings in particular about myself and my worth that was getting me into trouble. Thanks to this issue of the messages we learn from our family of origin – whether they are intended or not – I got the message a long time ago from my perfectionist mother that I wasn't good enough and I had grown up believing that to be a fact. And then I operated out in the world based on the fact that I was worthless – which was never true and yet was such a strong belief that it drove everything I did, everything I said, every thought, every action, and I created what I believed.

Here's the truth: if we can create a thought, we can stop a thought. In Chapter One we talked about neural pathways and how when presented with the same stimuli the thought automatically occurs and goes down the familiar pathway. We can change that. In my case I realised while I was in recovery that to truly move ahead I had to understand who I was, what wrong thinking was operating in me. I had to understand *who I was – not who I thought I was* based on the old messages that played in my brain. I needed to accept myself, and love myself. And this was no easy task. I had to focus on all of my thoughts and how they drove my behaviours. I had to begin to change them one by one.

The first thing I did was accept that everything I thought I knew was wrong, that I knew nothing. Deciding to operate this way – as if I knew nothing – was a blessing. I remember the first time I wanted to ask for something at the Recovery Centre. I wanted to go out with the group for a coffee in the morning, but my people-pleasing, doing other people's thinking for them habit meant my thoughts immediately went down the "I haven't been here long enough, they won't let me go...", etc. path. And I caught myself and decided to change it. Because really... I didn't know if they would let me go or not until I asked. So instead of believing I hadn't been there long enough and expecting them to say "no", I decided to just ask the question and suspend my expectations – if they said "no", that would be OK. But if they said "yes" then woo-hoo!! You can guess what they said... (and if you can't, they said "yes" and I went out for coffee with the others).

This practice of catching my thoughts and changing them from a negative "I know nothing" to suspending my expectations allowed me to stop creating those negative self-fulfilling prophecies because I wasn't going into situations with my beliefs. I was going in pretending I didn't have any beliefs or expectations one way or another. I was suspending judgment in my own mind... judgment about me, about them, about the situation, about the outcome. It allowed me to be open to seeing other ways of being and doing rather than forcing my way onto the situation because, after all, I knew my way brought me misery. I was ready to learn another way. And this learning another way changed the outcome of situations.

Through my understanding of the psychology of this, I came to realise that I am not a bad person – I just made bad choices. I began to understand that I did have some control over what happened in my life through changing my thoughts, my outlook, my behaviour and my beliefs about myself. I could re-wire my brain.

We Teach Others How to Treat Us

One of my most profound learnings around this self-fulfilling prophecy issue was that we teach others how to treat us. Our beliefs, our feelings about ourselves drive our actions and behaviours. If we feel we are worthless, stupid, fat or anything else, we will expect people to treat us this way, and they most likely will. Unfortunately, we don't always realise we're doing this.

For example, remember that I was raised with the belief that you should never do anything to upset anyone else? This meant never saying "no". So, every time someone asked me to do something, I said "yes," and even when I didn't want to say yes, I said it. After a while, my friends and colleagues learned that if they wanted something done, they could expect me to "help out" because I always agreed. The unfortunate part is that it didn't take very long for me to feel like I was being taken advantage of, and resentment set in. In truth, I had no right to be resentful. This was a situation that I created. I taught my friends and colleagues that I always said yes.

We teach spouses, friends, colleagues, our boss, and even our children how to treat us. I have a friend who provides a perfect example. When she wants something done around the house she asks once, and then asks again, and again… and after three times does the chore herself. What has her partner learned? That if he doesn't do it, she will. This leaves her feeling upset and angry because he appears to not listen or care.

I have recently experienced a most profound demonstration of the power of this. Years ago, I was in a relationship with someone I believed to be my soulmate. I was deeply in love with him. The problem was that neither of us had a great deal of self-esteem or confidence, and as a result we both had a serious drinking problem. His lack of self-esteem came out through anger and violence that was a "mask" or defence mechanism to cover the fact that he did not think he was worthy. I too hated myself. I felt like I didn't belong, like I was worthless, like there was something fundamentally wrong with me – and, of course, whatever we put out there we get back, and so in my hatred of myself I had attracted a person who felt the same about himself because like attracts like.

In my feeling so worthless, I always believed other people were right and I was wrong. I believed it was my job to make other people happy so they would like me (this sounds so sad to me now), and in this relationship that meant I needed to make him happy so he would love me. In his worthlessness, he needed to have control, he needed to always "look good" in action and in words, and since I was his girlfriend, that extended to me as I was nothing more than "property". A reflection on him.

Anyone smelling the potential for emotional abuse here? I hope so because that's exactly what happened only it wasn't just limited to emotional abuse. I lived for years being told how much to weigh, what to wear, where to work, how to wear my make-up, what to eat, when to eat… the list goes on and on. I was a puppet and because I felt I was worthless, I believed he was right, I believed I needed to comply so he would love me, I believed I was lucky to have him and I believed his control meant he loved me! (I just know you can all see the flaws in this thinking!) I felt that as long as he loved me I would be OK and did anything and everything I could to make him happy. Of course now I can see it for what it was. His control had nothing to do with his love for me – it was about him. And he couldn't have loved me because he didn't love himself. We were two broken people.

When I look back at this phase of my life, I now see it in a completely different light: would it have happened had I loved and respected myself the way I should have? I don't think so. It happened because I was open to it. I did not believe in, love, or trust myself. I felt so worthless that I took everyone else's opinion above my own. I created this self-fulfilling prophecy because I believed I was worthless and didn't deserve to be on this planet. I expected that if anyone loved me I would be lucky to have this and this belief drove my people-pleasing behaviour of obeying his commands and tolerating the abuse. Which, in turn, provided me the outcome I had expected all along which was that I'm worthless and the cycle continued.

This is not to say that this is true in all cases but it certainly was in mine. A most extreme example of the self-fulfilling prophecy. But still, it begs the question: what is your behaviour teaching others about how to treat you?

The Bottom Line

So, let's review: whatever we put out there is what we will get back. We create our own self-fulfilling prophecies based on our beliefs about ourselves, situations, circumstances, events and other people. Our beliefs drive our expectations. Our expectations then cause us to behave in certain ways, and our behaviour (based on our beliefs and expectations) then drive the outcome.

The good news is that we can turn this around. If we can create negative self-fulfilling prophecies, then we can create positive ones too using the same process. But our belief systems must change. For example: my old belief that "people like us don't become managers, or business owners..." As soon as I recognised that, I changed it to "people like me DO become managers and business owners and successful people". And as I started to believe it, my life started to change, I got promotions at work... one after the other, and eventually I started my own business – because I was no longer keeping myself locked in the prison of "people like me don't..."

What self-fulfilling prophecies are you currently running in your life?

- *What are your beliefs about yourself? About love? About work? Relationships? Family? The world and what is possible? Your future? What is your habitual thinking?*
- *How do those beliefs affect how you act, react, or interact with others?*
- *Are these outcomes good or bad? Which ones do you wish to change?*
- *What self-fulfilling prophecies are you creating through your own thoughts, feelings, and behaviour?*
- *What one belief, thought or behaviour can you start with to change the negative self-fulfilling prophecy into a positive one?*
- *How will you remember to do this? Remember this is about creating new thinking habits and you can't do it alone. You need a "mirror" to assist you.*
- *What is your commitment to yourself? When will you begin?*

SECRET #FOUR:

Your Secret Weapon: Confidence and Self-Esteem

"The story of the human race is the story of men and women selling themselves short."
Abraham Maslow

Success can be yours if you develop this one thing... self-esteem. And with self-esteem comes confidence. And this is your secret weapon.

Do you want to be happy? Be happy with yourself first! Wishing you were someone else, or had someone else's life isn't going to change anything. If you want to change the outside you must change the inside first. After 25 years of fighting this self-esteem battle myself I can tell you that it has nothing to do with anything out there in the world, rather it has everything to do with what goes on in your mind. For reasons we discussed in Chapter One about how our brains work, in Chapter Two about how we project our view of ourselves and the world onto other people and believe they see things the same way we do, and in Chapter Three about how those projections create self-fulfilling prophecies, we are the ones who stand in the way of our own happiness and success.

Whatever you want – happiness, peace of mind, more money, to lose weight, a better job, a better or different relationship – all of it starts with you and what goes on inside your mind! We must change our relationship with ourselves. We must update our opinion of ourselves! I'm sure you can tell, I am VERY passionate about this. I've had to do it, and continue to work on it, and I know the power of self-esteem. It's evident in my own life... if you've seen me speak, been to a workshop, or even just met me, you know this. I spent 20 years with "no fixed address", I was homeless, addicted, badly abused, I've been shot, stabbed, beaten to within an inch of my life and left on the side of the road for dead. And yet... here I am. Stronger and better than ever before. And by the way, I look much better now than I did when I was 25! Why? Because I've spent years working on my insides. Working to change the toxic thinking patterns I had learned as a child. Working to change those negative self-fulfilling prophecies into positive ones and it's worked. Today, I respect myself, I love myself and I appreciate myself.

People always ask me: "How did you get from a life on the street to where you are today?" The answer is simple: I developed my self-esteem and with that came confidence. The more I liked myself, the more confidence I had, and that allowed me to believe I deserved to be treated with respect, to have a job or career in line with my skills and talents. I could walk in the world and begin to believe I belonged and deserved happiness and all the good things life has to offer. And I continue to learn about myself – the good, the bad and everything in between and it has changed my opinion of myself and what is possible for me in this world. The answer to the "How did I get from there to here?" is simple. The work is not but it is the most important thing you can do for yourself or your children.

Remember that as a parent you are modelling for your children all kinds of things: how to have relationships, what confidence looks like, how to communicate, how to handle stress, how to manage emotions including anger, how to engage in conflict, how to be a friend, a partner... the list goes on and on. So even if you don't want to do this for yourself – do it for your children!!

And it's not just we who are reading this book but people of all ages, shapes, sizes, and socio-economic backgrounds who suffer with this one big affliction: low confidence and self-esteem. How do I know this? I see them and interact with them every day. In my career as a Professional Speaker and Trainer I work with thousands, and have worked with hundreds of thousands of people around the world, and what I see is talented, intelligent, beautiful people who are afraid, who hold themselves back, afraid to speak up, afraid to step into their greatness, to shine, to truly be who they are… and it breaks my heart. Why? Because I've been there, I know what it feels like, I was once in that place too.

I spent years being too afraid; too afraid of people not liking me, of being smarter than them, of hurting their feelings, of believing that there was something fundamentally wrong with me and that I was in no way good enough… good enough to walk among the good people I encountered. And all the while I was engaging in trying to control people, places, things and outcomes and the energy and time it took me in people-pleasing – trying to be all things to all people all the time – I was completely (as we all are) unaware of the damage I was doing to myself, my family, my children, my success at work, pretty much every aspect of my life was suffering, not the least of which was my health.

Self-awareness, self-esteem, that's what this is about and, to borrow a phrase from recovery circles, it works if you work it. There was a time I was terrified to get in an elevator if there were other people in it because it meant that, if I was getting off at the 3rd floor and they were going to a higher floor, I might have to ask someone to move to let me out and then they would notice me and probably get mad at me for disturbing them and putting them out and that paralysed me with fear. Who was I to ask these nice people to move out of my way? What right did I have? What if they got mad at me and said something not nice? What if they saw me for the worthless human being I was? No, it was easier to wait for an empty elevator or take the stairs, which is what I did.

For many, many years, even for the first few years I was in recovery, I didn't know what anyone looked like but I knew what kind of shoes they wore. That's how I identified people… by their shoes. Why? Because I was too ashamed of myself, I was too worthless to look people in the eye so I walked around looking at the ground… and all I saw were people's feet. It's funny when I think about it now, but nonetheless, it's the truth. I hated myself so much that I didn't believe I deserved to be around people. And I was sure that if I looked them in the eye they would see that. And I believe some of them probably would have seen how much I hated myself, much like I can see it in others now.

I often tell this story in my workshops and people can't believe it's true because you would never know it to speak with me today – but I assure you it is true. I could not even walk through a shopping mall I was so aware of people looking at me, and afraid they could see the "worthless" sign I believed was tattooed on my forehead. That's how I know my techniques work. Because I felt so worthless I was afraid to ask for help so I had to do this on my own. What I want to share with you are the techniques and lessons I learned while developing my own self-esteem and confidence, and if they worked for me in that state… I know they will work for you.

But first we should talk about what self-esteem is exactly. I know for me, the term was very confusing. I knew I needed it… I knew successful people had it… but I didn't know what it was. How could someone love themselves and what exactly does that mean?

Confidence & Self Esteem: What it is

Power comes from confidence and self-esteem. It's your base, your foundation, and without it you have nothing to work from. This is where personal power comes from and if you have taken any kind of Leadership or Influencing training, you are familiar with this term.

What is confidence and self-esteem? In psychology, self-esteem is described as a person's overall sense of self-worth or personal value. It is feeling effective as a person. Confidence is defined as a belief in your own abilities: self-assurance or a belief in your ability to succeed. Increased confidence comes from increased self-esteem. The more you love and value yourself, the more confidence you have in your choices, opinions, actions and ideas. And that's the point of this book… you must love, respect and value yourself first. If you do, the rest will start to fall into place.

Self-esteem and confidence are the source from which you inspire others, it is where inner strength comes from, where courage comes from. You can't have courage without fear, but courage is feeling the fear and trusting yourself to handle whatever comes your way. Believing in yourself, your talents, your abilities, believing that you are worthy, unique, lovable and capable, believing that you belong on this planet and deserve to be here – this is self-esteem. Believing that you deserve the best that life, love, and work have to offer. Believing that you are good, life is good, and you are capable of handling anything that comes your way. Knowing and loving yourself, faults and all… this is self-esteem, and this is where confidence comes from and this is the source of everything – your secret weapon.

No one can love you, no one can believe in you, no one can respect you if you don't love, believe in, and respect yourself. That's the big secret. Again, it doesn't come from outside. I don't believe there is such a thing as luck, I believe we attract what comes our way – either good or bad things. So, if you're attracting things you don't want, you need to look inside to find out why. We'll talk more about attraction and manifesting later in the book, but for now let's work on your power base.

Success lies in this internal foundation of confidence and self-esteem. If you look at truly successful people, they are successful because they believed in their dreams, they have confidence in themselves, they do not focus on what could go wrong, but rather, on what could go right. Let me tell you a story about a rather tenacious chipmunk that demonstrates how this works: The other day as I was gazing out into my backyard I witnessed something that caused me to pause – I saw a chipmunk, maybe 3" long and very tiny, go head-to-head with a big black squirrel three or four times his size, fighting over who was going to win the right to feed on the peanuts I leave in the birdfeeder. I watched this, marvelling at the ferocity of the tiny chipmunk. He just was not giving up. He took on this black squirrel and he won. The squirrel ran away, and the tiny chipmunk jumped up onto the feeder and commenced filling his cheeks with his prize.

As I stood there watching this, it occurred to me that this chipmunk had provided a very important lesson: he won. His opponent was bigger, stronger and weighed a lot more but the chipmunk still took him on and won. Why? Because the chipmunk didn't know that he couldn't win. As an animal, he doesn't have the ability like we humans do to know that the odds are against him. He wanted the food, and the squirrel was in his way. The chipmunk won because the chipmunk doesn't have the capacity to know that he shouldn't have won.

Think about it... if the chipmunk were human, what would it have thought? It would have thought that the squirrel was so much larger and heavier, and logic would have dictated that the squirrel would win. The chipmunk might have even thought: "I'll never win so why even try", or "Who do I think I am taking on a big squirrel?" I'm wondering if any of this sounds familiar to you? Because this is what we do, we focus on all those things that could go wrong instead of keeping our eye on what we desire and believing in our ability to achieve it. Our very human ability to rationalise and apply logic often prevents us from going after the very things we say we want. We believe that we don't deserve it, or it will never happen, or, we will fail. And instead of trying... instead of working toward what we want, we give up before we even start. I do believe we should be like that chipmunk... that chipmunk won because it didn't know it couldn't.

You will see this same example with successful people. They continue to learn and grow, they continue to move forward in love, life, and career. They do not let mistakes or failure take them out of the game. They fall down, they get up, dust themselves off, and go back at it. This is self-esteem: knowing that a mis-step or a mistake is nothing more than a learning experience, knowing and believing that they have what it takes to achieve their dreams. This is confidence. And this, my dear friends, is what we could all use a boost in!

Have you ever been with someone who didn't like themselves very much? Always talking badly about themselves? Have you ever been around someone who lacked confidence? Talented, smart, but didn't believe they could do anything? Maybe it's you? It's frustrating!

In the chapter on self-fulfilling prophecies I demonstrated how we attract that which we believe. Believe you are worthless and undeserving and you will attract relationships with people who think *they* are worthless and undeserving. Believe you are not deserving of receiving love and you will attract relationships with people who are incapable of loving you. Believe you are not good enough, not talented enough, not smart enough and you will attract jobs that are unfulfilling. Because this is how it works. Whatever you are feeling on the inside is sending energy out into the world and you are attracting that back to you. Like attracts like.

How High Is Your Self-Esteem?

All of us can use a boost in confidence and self-esteem. Some more than others. According to *The Self Esteem Book* by Joe Rubino approximately 85% of the world's population suffers with low self-esteem! Low self-esteem is the universal common denominator among all people with addictions to any mind-altering substances. In a study conducted in Britain on teenage mothers, they found that 85-90% of the teenage mothers opted to keep their babies rather than give them up for adoption because they believed that the baby would provide the kind of unconditional love that they never had. In the US, approximately 7 in 10 girls believe they are not good enough or do not measure up in some way including their looks, performance in school, and relationships. Only 2% of women think they're beautiful. One out of four college-aged women have an eating disorder. The statistics on this are horrible!

In my experience of speaking and doing workshops around the world I meet people every day who are smart and talented and yet believe that they are "less than". I believe that we all carry around some degree of worthlessness – that is, a secret belief that we are not good enough. For some people, it's just a small voice that pops up every once in a while; for others, it's the voice that speaks the loudest in their minds, driving every conscious thought, every action, and every decision they make. Take it from someone who was one of those "worthless" cases – this takes a lot of energy!! So, the goal is to quiet the voice, get it to a place where it's a small voice, a quiet voice and not a guiding force in your life.

How do you know if your self-esteem is low? Well, if you were drawn to buy this book then I would suggest there is a need to boost your own confidence and self-esteem. Or maybe you are feeling stuck and want to make changes in your life but are afraid, or don't know how. This is also a sign that you need a little boost.

Here are some questions to ask yourself, some other warning signs that your level of self-esteem and confidence may be getting in the way of your happiness, peace of mind and success.

- *Are you controlled by fear, anxiety and depression?*
- *Do you find yourself constantly evaluating what other people think of you?*
- *Do you think of yourself as being inadequate or unacceptable?*
- *Do you feel unloved or unlovable?*
- *Are you fearful of failing, of making a mistake that others might see?*
- *Do you lack confidence in your ability to do more, or to make decisions?*
- *Are you unable to build or maintain healthy relationships? (Do you even know what a healthy relationship is?)*
- *Are you devastated by rejection, disapproval or criticism? Do you avoid situations that might result in these things?*
- *Are you afraid of change?*

Your relationships can also be mirrors. What we see in others that we don't like is often a reflection of ourselves. Do you find yourself attracting people with low self-esteem or a lack of confidence? Do people in your personal life treat you with less respect than you would like? This is also telling you something.

You Are Not Alone...

As I have said, it's not just you. We've all read articles and seen the television talk shows where women keep complaining about attracting "losers" and wanting to know how to change that. And I told you the story of me, terrified of people so much that I couldn't get in an elevator or go to a crowded mall. I wouldn't even return anything to a store if it was defective because I was so afraid they would get mad at me and turn me away and I'd be marked forever! And there are others, plenty of others.

I have a friend who started out as a participant in a seminar I was offering and bought a couple of my programs. She then became a coaching client and eventually a friend. She is highly educated and works for a very large global organisation as an executive in a high-ranking and very important position. And she hated herself. Her feelings about herself were so strong, she was so sure that she was a bad person that she pushed everyone away, not believing she was worth their time and attention. She always looked unhappy, she was sarcastic and sharp with people, always pointing out their mistakes, she talked down to people, treating them as if they were stupid, all to protect herself (in her own mind) from other people finding out how worthless she was.

Eventually, she became so hard to work with that people would constantly complain about her and she was always in trouble with her boss and Human Resources. But she kept her job. Why? Because she is smart and very talented and extremely knowledgeable and capable in what she does. She is really good at her job and everyone knows it – everyone except her. She couldn't see that, she was blinded by her own self-loathing.

Another person I know, again extremely smart and incredibly talented, has got one of the happiest dispositions of anyone I have ever met, and he's funny and very sociable! He's also one of those people who is good at anything he tries and succeeds at anything he puts his mind to. He's always been this way. He also, due to some circumstances in his early family life, feels like he is worthless, like he doesn't belong and so he hides. He has spent his whole life either not working, or working at menial jobs because he is afraid he is not good enough, not capable and not worthy of love. All the amazing things he is capable of are kept to himself out of fear that they will not be good enough for others, that he will be rejected. All this talent hidden from the world. Basically wasted. It breaks my heart.

I was in Europe conducting a workshop and there was a woman who again, same story, knew all the right answers, was educated and experienced in her field and yet terrified to speak up. She had no confidence in herself, and even with her experience, her knowledge, and her talent she stayed in the background, afraid to draw attention to herself. And so she was constantly overlooked at work as not having the ability or the knowledge to take on tasks and responsibilities. She stayed stuck in a low-level job when in fact she was the most capable in the department. More capable than her boss… but no one knew it, not even her.

This is a common story and it's one I'd like to change. I'm hoping you want to change this too… at least for yourself.

So, at this point you might be asking: "But how does this happen?" How do smart, talented, wonderful human beings end up feeling unlovable, unworthy, incapable of managing in this world? This is the importance of the first chapter on how our brain works and the power of conditioning. Who knows what was said, or done… but somehow, something maybe a long time ago, or not such a long time ago, caused you to believe that you were less than, that you were unworthy, unlovable, or incapable… or, as in my case, maybe all three. I can trace it back to my early childhood and the unwritten messages and rules in my house. Maybe you can too… maybe it was your father who only ever yelled at you, or maybe you were overweight as a child and were teased and still carry that self-image around with you. As I have said in previous chapters – these experiences imprint themselves in our subconscious and those imprints go on to drive our beliefs about ourselves, our lives, our relationships, our jobs, and the world. We act and react from that original state. We are locked in the invisible prison in our mind. Once again here's that great quote from Abraham Maslow:

> *"Every act or thought, every one without exception, records itself in our unconscious and makes us despise or love ourselves more."*

So back to the self-fulfilling prophecy: if at some point in the past we got the message that we didn't fit in, or were different, or stupid, or not good enough, it may have imprinted. You may still be viewing the world and operating from that Centre of the Universe… and that's what needs to change. I do remember my father saying to me: "If you continue this way no man will ever want to marry you…", (a very 1950's thing to say for sure) and it stuck. I can't even tell you the damage that did! Because I believed no one would ever want to marry me I sabotaged every relationship I was in. I've been engaged seven times. Yes, seven. I have an engagement ring museum! I didn't get married until I was 41 years old... that's how long it took me to clear that one! I can laugh about it now but that's the power of our subconscious, that's why we need to work on re-wiring our thought processes.

I'm hoping that by now you have taken the time to read and complete the reflection questions in the first three Chapters, to start to identify the messages you carry with you, identify the faulty thinking that guides your daily activities.

Everyone suffers with lack of confidence or dwindling self-esteem at some time in their lives. No one is immune to this, it's just that, for some of us this is an ongoing issue. One that gets in the way of our happiness, our joy, our financial well-being, and our success in general and it keeps us locked in that invisible prison. Sometimes, as in my case, it's old – as old as I am. I just never grew up with any... right from the start this was my one big lesson in life.

For others among you, it might be a situation or event that has triggered it and caused you to question yourself ever since. Maybe you were the kid in school who never got picked for the team, or always got picked last; maybe your high school boyfriend broke up with you because he said you were fat or found someone prettier, or maybe an authority figure told you that you would never amount to anything. Who knows where it comes from – I hear all kinds of stories from people. There is no right or wrong here. If it's a big deal to you then it's a big deal.

When it happened doesn't matter – it happened. The circumstances are often different, but the feelings are the same. And now, it's up to you to do something about it!

How to Move Forward

As we have discussed in this chapter, *we* keep ourselves locked in that invisible prison. Our belief systems, old and outdated, prevent us from taking risks, trying new things, or making changes.

This is why you need to look, really, honestly, and take inventory of what's there. You need to look deeply into yourself and your belief systems. Only then can you know where to begin, only then can you start to move out from the shadows of your past, break away from your conditioning and start to move forward in your life!

And yes, before you ask, anyone can do this. All you have to do is try! But you can't half try. You have to completely surrender yourself to the process and jump in with both feet – heck, jump in with your whole being!

Sometimes I know (because I'm also guilty of it) we think "OK, I'll give this a try and see if it works", but what we really mean is we'll stick our toe in, and when it feels uncomfortable we'll pull it out and say: "Well, that's not going to work!" And of course it won't – we didn't give it a chance!

Lack of discomfort is a sure sign of a half-way effort and that's OK, because when the pain of your existence outweighs the fear of change you will be ready and you will try again. That's the nice thing about this – you can start anytime. Anyone can do this and you are never too old! So keep reading, even if you only take one or two techniques to try... it's a start and it will help, and something is better than nothing.

As I write this I can feel some of you saying: "Sounds great... for you... but what if I can't change?", "What if I'm too old and set in my ways?", and my personal favourite: "I can't help it, this is the way I am!" Yes. This may be the way you are now and the way you have been, but you can change. The story you tell yourself is false. All you have to do is want to and believe you can. Believe you can or believe you can't. Either way, you are correct.

This is how you start. You choose to believe you can! Your body will follow what your brain tells it to do. Tell yourself you can't change and you won't. Tell yourself you can and the door is magically open for those changes to occur! Neuroscience has proven that unlike other parts of our body, the brain does not lose neuroplasticity as we age. Meaning, we are *never* too old to learn something new.

You must let go of the story you tell yourself and now is the time. You are not your story. "This is the way I am" is a story. "I'm too old, too fat, too stupid, too worthless" is a story. "I've been this way for too long now, I'm too set in my ways" is a story. It's not true. You might believe it to be true but I'm telling you it's not! So let it go, drop it, imagine it is a big fluffy sweater you have been wearing and the sun has now come out and you are hot! The sweat is pouring down your face, your neck, down your back... it's uncomfortable wearing this fluffy sweater. It no longer fits. It's weighing you down. You need to take off the sweater.

Imagine yourself taking off the sweater... the sweater that holds your doubts, fears, and insecurities. Now see yourself folding it neatly and put it away. Because here's the thing about this: you can have your old fluffy sweater of doubt back any time you like! If you give this new, lighter way of living a chance, I don't think you'll want your old sweater back, but it's there for you... just in case.

We are all responsible for our own behaviour. It's the only thing we can control in this crazy world and it's all about choices. When I don't make the right choices, I experience some kind of emotional pain or discomfort, and sometimes, with me as with others, it's physical pain as well. This is what my addiction was about, but looking at the pain would have meant identifying choices and doing what I considered to be very difficult, or even impossible things – so it was easier to escape reality, to escape the pain with my addictions.

We all do this... we're not happy, we know we can't continue this way whether it be in a job, a relationship, or in ourselves but we don't believe there is a way out or can't see a comfortable way out and so we find ways to escape... drugs, alcohol, food, shopping, perfectionism, control, worry, sex... there are many things we use to escape.

This is about facing the reality of who we are and making different choices. And when we make different choices then different things start to happen. Better things, more positive things. And we always have a choice – you may think you don't, but you do. When we say we "don't have a choice" what that really means is that we do have a choice, we just don't like the choices and so we stay stuck. It's like saying "I can't", which, because we have this thing called free will and we are the only ones who can control our thoughts, feelings, and behaviours, really means "I won't" because you can and you would if you really wanted to!

So choose! Choose you! Choose to start loving yourself, believing in yourself, valuing yourself! You will attract better relationships and jobs, more money and abundance in all areas. This is your secret weapon for success!

Let's Have a Reality Check

If you think I'm overstating this fact about self-esteem and confidence, I'm not. I know what it's like to be completely without confidence or anything remotely resembling self-esteem, and I know what it's like when you uncover the secret – the inner strength that we all have. Here's a partial list of benefits that I have received through developing my self-esteem and confidence and you can reap these same benefits and more by following the suggestions in this book:

- *More self-esteem and confidence to ask for what I want – and get it.*
- *A successful career doing something I love and is uniquely suited to me.*
- *Improved physical health – no more migraine headaches, no more breathing problems, no more anxiety attacks. I lost weight because I didn't engage in emotional eating anymore, I no longer had the desire to avoid my feelings through using alcohol, drugs, gambling or anything else. I didn't get sick as often.*
- *Improved emotional health – I slept better because I didn't toss and turn all night worrying about situations and relationships and replaying conversations in my head. I had less stress overall, less worry, less anxiety.*
- *Quality of life improved as a result of my physical and emotional health improving. Relationships became easier and more enjoyable.*
- *No more needing to people-please.*
- *No more need to "control" my life, or other people's lives.*
- *No more being taken advantage of.*
- *Began to believe I deserved happiness and success.*
- *I felt better, I looked better, I began to age... backwards!!*
- *Increased respect. I was able to teach people how I wanted to be treated.*
- *More energy, more focus, more joy, more money, more everything...*

I could go on and on. Like I said, this is a partial list. And all of this because I bought a book. It didn't cost me any money. I did not go to therapy. I simply bought a book... and that's what this book is about. These are the techniques I used, the knowledge I gained and the changes I made that allowed me to go from addicted, abused and living on the streets to the success I enjoy today. And I'm sharing them with you because anyone can do this and be successful at it. You just have to want to.

Whenever people ask me a question after they hear or read my story, it's "How did you get from there to here?" It never fails. And whenever they ask the question I can always feel the underlying intent, the words they are not saying. Because after all, "However did you get from there to here?" is a very safe way of saying: "I'm not happy with my life, there is something wrong, I'm afraid there is something really wrong with me, I'm a mistake, I don't feel good enough, lovable enough, I don't belong here" or any other of the deeply held pains that you are likely feeling if you are reading this book.

So I always know what they mean when they ask the question – they are asking me to tell them how I did it so they can do it too. So here it is, everything I did to get to where I am today and all the things I learned along the way. And I do believe that if I did it, so can you.

Here's the check-up again. Which of these statements do you identify with?

- *Are you controlled by fear, anxiety and depression?*
- *Do you find yourself constantly evaluating what other people think of you?*
- *Do you think of yourself as being inadequate or unacceptable?*
- *Do you feel unloved or unlovable?*
- *Are you fearful of failing, of making a mistake that others might see?*
- *Do you lack confidence in your ability to do more, or to make decisions?*
- *Are you unable to build or maintain healthy relationships? (Do you even know what a healthy relationship is?)*
- *Are you devastated by rejection, disapproval or criticism? Do you avoid situations that might result in these things?*
- *Are you afraid of change?*

Which are the three biggest issues for you?

1. _____

_____

2. _____

_____

3. _____

_____

What might happen if you were to start to feel better and more confident in these areas?

On a scale of 1 – 10 (1 being the lowest, 10 the highest) how willing are you to begin to work on these areas?

If you're not already at a 9 or 10, what will it take to increase your commitment to yourself?

SECRET #FIVE:

Five Proven Techniques for Developing Self-Esteem

"Self-esteem is the reputation we acquire with ourselves."
"Self-esteem is a powerful force within each of us…
Self-esteem is the experience that we are appropriate
to life and to the requirements of life."
Nathaniel Branden

Health, happiness, better relationships with your significant other, friends, family, children, the population at large, more money, increased success in general… the benefits to developing your self-esteem are many and they are not one-time benefits, they continue to grow and give. Things get bigger and better as your self-esteem gets bigger and better. Your confidence rises. People start to treat you differently. Opportunities arise. Trust me – I've experienced this. When I started this journey to develop my self-esteem and, by extension, my confidence, I was working in a ladies clothing shop making minimum wage. As my self-esteem grew, as my confidence grew, so did my pay cheque. And it continues to grow as I do, 25 years and it hasn't stopped yet, nor do I expect it to, as long as I don't stop.

I laugh sometimes because I can look back and chart my growth, my progress through looking at my jobs, my pay cheque, my relationships, my friends and activities, even my holidays. The more confidence and self-esteem I developed the more opportunities that opened up for me and it will be the same for you. We limit ourselves with our own ideas of what is and is not possible for us when the truth is… you don't know what's possible.

I took the journey to develop my self-esteem, and with that my confidence grew, and with that my life grew. I committed myself and jumped in with both feet and here I am. And now, here you are. So the question becomes: what are you going to do?

One step at a time. That's how this works. One foot in front of the other, and a commitment to continually learn about yourself every day. We have a habit of keeping ourselves stuck by staying in our comfort zone – sticking to what we know, what is safe. This is how we think we are protecting ourselves, but as I shared about the self-fulfilling prophecy, all it does is get us more of the same. If we truly want to change, if you really want your life to be different, then YOU have to change… how you think, how you behave, how you respond to people, places and things. Start by doing one thing differently every day. Take a risk every day, even a small one. The idea is to prove to yourself that you are not as fragile, hopeless or worthless as you think you are. It doesn't matter what it is: try a new restaurant, drive a different way to work or to the grocery shop, instead of yelling at your kids for not cleaning their room try calmly asking them, or explaining why you need them to tidy their room, and then walk away. You may be uncomfortable when you do something differently but that's the point – discomfort doesn't mean something is wrong, it means something is different. We always feel discomfort when we are stretching ourselves to learn something new, and you my dear readers are taking the first step in developing your self-esteem and confidence and changing your life!

Just by driving to work a different way? Yes! Because you are waking up from the sleep you have been in, you are coming out of the numbness. You know how your arm or your leg tingles when you move it after it's fallen asleep? Well, the discomfort is you tingling after waking yourself up from being asleep so to speak!

Techniques for Developing Self-Esteem

I think I've been transparent about saying this issue of self-esteem has been, is, and will continue to be, my lifelong battle. It wasn't until I was in rehab I became aware that there was something called self-esteem and that "real people" had it and I knew that I did not. I didn't know what it was, I just knew I needed to get some, and so the first thing I did when I got out of re-hab was buy two books. The first one was John Bradshaw's *Homecoming* because I had seen John on a Televison Special while in rehab (because nothing ever happens by accident in this life). He was talking about family cycles and how we learn what we live and then we live what we learn thereby perpetuating the cycle.

This really resonated with me, this man spoke to me – it was my first clue in unravelling the mess I had made of my life. The internet was then in its infancy and so my only course of action was to obtain one of his books and since *Homecoming* was the title of the Television Special, I bought that one. Today, of course, you can go to John's website www.bradshawmedia.com and buy DVDs and books and CDs and all sorts of things – which I highly recommend you do! I always credit John Bradshaw with saving my life.

The second book I bought was Nathaniel Brandon's *Self-Esteem* because I knew I needed this self-esteem thing but I needed to know what it was first! Now I'd be lying to you if I told you that I read these books cover to cover – I didn't, but only because I didn't need to. From the self-esteem book, I learned that self-esteem is feeling effective as a person – which I did not. So that was it, I needed to learn to be effective as a person. It also meant loving yourself – which I did not – and respecting yourself – which I obviously did not!

From John's book, I saw all the "unwritten" messages I had received from my parents. I saw the control, the perfectionism, the people-pleasing that my mother demonstrated, I saw how my parents conducted their relationship, and while I knew all of this, I saw for the first time the behaviours they had modelled for me and how I was behaving the same way – repeating that cycle. I also saw for the very first time how I also possessed all the same characteristics and behaviours I said I did not like about my mother and how I engaged in all the behaviours that I thought were so wrong with my parents' relationship!

It goes without saying I did not like these realisations very much! It was very hard to swallow, but this would be my first step in developing my self-awareness. I knew I did not want to behave like this, and from reading John's book, I knew these behaviours were not healthy and so this is where I decided to start.

I made a list of all the things I didn't like about myself using my family as a mirror. Then I prioritised them in order of importance for me to work on. Numbers one, two, and three on that list were self-esteem, people-pleasing and perfectionism (needing to be perfect in all things otherwise a policeman would come and take me away – geez… that even sounds like a two-year old's view, doesn't it?) This is where I started.

I know for myself, when I read John Bradshaw's *Homecoming* in 1991, it was the springboard for my developing my self-esteem and it was ever so slightly raised just from reading the book! How? Because what I realised is that I was not necessarily worthless as a person, there were circumstances that had contributed to me ending up where I was in my life and they were circumstances I had no control over (my conditioning). It was not entirely my fault, although **it was my responsibility to fix it**. John Bradshaw himself did not raise my self-esteem (although as I said, I do credit him with saving my life), he just wrote the book. It was my choice to read it, my choice to internalise it, think about it, learn from it and apply it to my own life. That's how I raised my self-esteem. And that's how I'm hoping you'll raise yours. So let's start…

TECHNIQUE 1: **SELF-AWARENESS**

This, to me, is a foundational technique. It's the importance of all the chapters before this one. Looking deeply into yourself, your conditioning, the unwritten rules and messages you were raised with that still guide your life to this day. How you feel about yourself, your life, the world. What's operating in you?

If you're thinking: "This already sounds hard. It sounds like too much work", the answer is yes... and no. Yes, becoming aware of what's operating in you (Chapters 2 and 3) and constantly being aware of what's happening inside yourself, being aware of your feelings and where they are coming from – what subconscious buttons have been pushed – watching how you act and react to people and situations does take discipline and it takes time to develop the habit. But once you have it, it becomes part of you – this is called "dual awareness". Most of us never stop to think about what we do or say and why we do or say it, but remember what I said in Chapter 2 about the Centre of the Universe? Whatever you are doing or saying is all about you! It's not what happens to you, it's how you react to it. The only way you will ever unravel the mystery of you is to observe yourself, study yourself. Find out what you like, what you're good at, and what you don't like, what you're not good at, and what you don't like, you can fix! This is the great gift of being human. We can change our thoughts, emotions, behaviours and in doing so, we start to increase our confidence and self-esteem and all you have to do is try.

> *"Human beings can alter their lives by altering their attitudes of mind."*
> **William James**

Try this: the next time you are stuck in traffic, having an argument with your partner, yelling at your kids, upset with your friend, feeling less than, anything really – watch yourself, observe yourself, study yourself under the microscope of your mind. Ask yourself why? What are you feeling? Where is this coming from? What is really going on? Whose voice is in your head? Yours? Your mother's? The voice of fear? Or the voice that wants to keep you stuck where you are because at least it's safe and you know what to expect? What button is being pushed? Are you feeling worthless, wrong, disrespected, different? What is happening in you?

This is the fundamental practice of self-awareness. Of recognising in yourself what is happening... what button is being pushed... which of the old tapes is playing... what is causing the thought, feeling, behaviour. Trace it back... see if you can identify its origins. If you can, then you can deal with it rationally. You can think about it and recognise if it is accurate, if it is appropriate, and if it is helping you and your peace of mind, happiness, relationships and success, or... if it's preventing one or all of these things.

If you're scratching your head right now wondering how you can be focused on doing things while watching yourself do things, let me explain: this takes no time and a lot of time all at the same time. Confused yet? It takes as much time as you want to give it. Your brain is a powerful tool, capable of a great many things and one of them is that we have the ability to observe ourselves as we go through our day. Have you ever found yourself thinking many things at once? Or how about driving down the street while thinking about what you need from the grocery store or replaying a conversation you just had or planning your vacation? This is the same premise. You observe yourself going about your day. It takes no time away from your daily activities but a lot of time in engaging part of your brain to observe yourself. Dual awareness, one part of your brain is actively at work going through the day-to-day motions and conversations while the other part is observing it. No time and a lot of time all at the same time.

You can practise this anytime, anywhere. It's similar if not the same as the practice you may have been reading about lately in magazines and newspapers that is showing so much promise – mindfulness, only when I started practising this it didn't have a name!

This practice will allow you to understand what's operating in you. What are your buttons, how do you keep yourself locked in your invisible prison? When you can figure that out, you can fix it!

1. *Stop right now and look inside... how are you feeling right now?*
2. *What is happening inside of you? As you were reading this chapter what were/are you feeling?*
3. *What is your inside voice telling you? Whose voice is it? Where is it coming from? You? Or the "committee" of people who contributed to your conditioning?*

PART ONE: SECRET #FIVE: FIVE PROVEN TECHNIQUES FOR DEVELOPING SELF-ESTEEM

TECHNIQUE 2: **SELF-ESTEEM CHECK**

This technique is a barometer that I've used for a long time. I first did it when I was in rehab. The exercise is very simple: list 10 reasons why someone would want to be your friend.

That's it. Sounds simple. Take some time now and make a list... 10 reasons why someone would want to be your friend.

1. _____
2. _____
3. _____
4. _____
5. _____
6. _____
7. _____
8. _____
9. _____
10. _____

How did you do? The first time I did this activity I could not find one single reason why someone would want to be my friend, so I'd say if you came up with 2 or 3 you're doing better than I did the first time! If you managed to come up with 6 or 7 you're doing great! Of course the goal is to come up with 10 and that's why it's been my barometer. I still do this exercise every once in a while to see how I'm doing, to chart my progress.

I do remember in rehab though, I couldn't come up with anything. Others had things on their list: one man said people would want to be his friend because he had a pool in his backyard. I didn't have a pool. I didn't even have anywhere to live. One person said she was a good cook! I couldn't cook. I didn't even know how to clean. I couldn't operate a vacuum cleaner. Someone else said they had a good job (before they lost it) so people would want to be their friend because they once had a good job. I'm afraid we were a sad group of people that we couldn't come up with any valid reasons why people would want to be our friends… I was worst of all. I had nothing on my list.

So… how many do you have? Let's work on getting it to 10!

TECHNIQUE 3: UPDATE YOUR OPINION OF YOURSELF

This is one of the reasons I knew I had to work on this. I truly could not think of any reason why someone would want to be my friend but I could come up with plenty of reasons why they wouldn't. It was time to tip the scales. I was determined to get some of this "self-esteem" that they all talked about. But I didn't know how… I did know that while I was in rehab miraculous things had happened to me.

You recall how the day before I quit drinking I had got drunk, called my boss at the shop and quit my job? Well, about three weeks into rehab I received a letter from that boss.

What makes this the first miracle is that I had not told anyone but my boyfriend and my father where I was going. I didn't know the name of the hospital or the address, so basically all they knew is that I was somewhere in California in rehab. And yet… here was a letter from my boss.

Here's the second miracle because it said that: "If this is the kind of employee you are when you have problems, then I can only imagine how great you will be when you return. I do not accept your resignation. Instead, we are putting you on full medical leave. You will continue to receive compensation while you are away and when you're ready, your job will be here waiting for you." I was dumbfounded. I cried for days. I couldn't believe it… not only did I still have a job but they were paying me while I was in the hospital? It was beyond anything I could have predicted or imagined might happen. And it got me wondering… what was it that made me such a good employee? I clearly could not find reasons why someone would want me around and yet my boss did. And then I started to recognise that I still had friends. I may not have been able to identify why, but I had friends. And I had a boyfriend. And my family still talked to me. This was confusing to me, so I decided that when I left rehab I would find out why.

Here's the exercise I created for myself. It works. It worked for me, it's worked for thousands of my clients since, and it will work for you. But fair warning, it takes courage.

STEP ONE: Identify three people in your life you trust.

STEP TWO: Ask each of these people why they are your friend or any variation of that. I asked my friends for three reasons they were my friend. Three things they liked about me. I asked my boss and my co-workers for three things that made me a good employee. You can ask anything: what are their three favourite qualities of yours? What are the three things you are most good at? It doesn't matter. The point is, you don't have an accurate opinion of yourself. It's outdated. You have to ask others for their view – how do they see you? What do they like and admire about you? You could ask 10 people for one word they would use to describe you. There are many ways you can do this, but the point is, you have to see yourself through others' eyes.

STEP THREE: This is hard – don't TALK. Just listen to what they say. Don't justify, don't argue, don't diminish. Just listen and write down what they say and thank them for sharing it with you.

STEP FOUR: Look for themes. I'll bet people say the same thing. This is what you need to pay attention to. Don't argue in your head, don't tell yourself reasons why it's not true. Just read what was said and find themes.
A note here: this may be a very difficult activity. Because of our Centre of the Universe orientation and how long you have held your opinion of yourself it's hard to believe what others say. If you need to, ask for clarification.

Ask for an example. I suggest this activity to all the people I work with, and for a lot of them, they get feedback that they find very difficult to believe and easy to ignore.

One client is very good with networking and connections, however she herself thinks she can't speak to people.

She still, after two years, finds it difficult to understand how this is true about her. But it IS true about her.

She just doesn't see it. That's why we need to update our opinion of ourselves. Our opinions are often not accurate. We must believe others and how they see us.

STEP FIVE: Every day choose one word, one theme to focus on.
As you go through your day look for evidence that what was said is true. As I have written about, it is our habit to find proof that what WE believe is true. If you believe (like I did) that you're worthless and you don't belong, then you will only pay attention to the proof of that. This activity forces your mind to pay attention to things you wouldn't normally notice.

Each day, choose a different word or theme. Or maybe you want to choose one word or theme for a week. That's fine. The point is that you start to see the good things about yourself and looking for proof forces you to realise that they are true.

Do this for 30 days and you will see your self-esteem rise.

I used this exercise for months and months at a time. Believe me when I say it was hard for me to go to these people, feeling as worthless as I did, and ask: "Why are you my friend?" or "What makes me a good employee?" In all cases the people I asked looked at me like I was crazy! Like the question was ridiculous... because in their mind it was. But it's not their mind I was trying to re-wire, it was mine! When I asked my boss she said: "You're kidding right?" I responded... looking at the ground... "No. I really want to know, what are three things that make me a good employee?" She gave me eight things. As did everyone. I asked for three and I got six or eight or ten in some cases. Things I would never have imagined. Things I found very hard to believe. One friend said I was "generous". Well in my mind that was ridiculous! I had no money. How could I be generous?

But that's not what she meant. She meant generous with my time, with my help, sharing knowledge and information. When I understood this, I started to notice... I WAS generous with these things! And once again, my self-esteem rose ever so slightly. I now had one thing on my list of 10 reasons someone would want to be my friend.

I have said all along that this is about re-wiring your brain. Overcoming faulty thinking habits. We cannot see ourselves as others see us. We only see ourselves through the lens of our thoughts, feelings, actions, deeds and misdeeds. And we interact with the world as though they are also seeing us through that lens. They are not. They see something completely different and you need to understand what that is and then find the proof that what they are saying is true. This will begin to re-wire your brain.

1. **What three people will you ask?**

    a. *Name:*   *Relationship:*

    _____

    What question will you ask them?

    _____

    b. *Name:*   *Relationship*

    _____

    What question will you ask them?

    _____

    c. *Name:*   *Relationship:*

    _____

    What question will you ask them?

    _____

2. **When will you commit to start?** _____

3. **Who will you start with?** _____

TECHNIQUE 4: EVENING SELF-REFLECTION

This is another powerful technique in re-wiring your brain. At the end of each day, before you go to bed sit somewhere quiet and reflect on your day. Instead of our usual habit of focusing on all the things that went wrong or that we did wrong that day, find at least three things that you did right!

You can write them down in a journal, but each night reflect back on your day and identify three things you did well, or that you are proud of. These don't have to be big things… it can be as simple as I got out of bed on time this morning. Or, today I stopped to talk to someone and ask how they were doing. It might be today, I caught myself beating myself up and I stopped, or I shut down the negative self-talk when I made a mistake at work.

I know when I started doing this, some days I would kneel beside my bed and scan my day and the only thing I could find would be things like "I did a really good job of being an adult today", or "I didn't take it personally when so'n'so made that nasty comment". It doesn't matter what it is, big or small, just find three things you did well that day and resist the urge to say: "Yes but I did 23 things wrong". This isn't about what you did wrong, it's about finding those things you did right. If you can do this consistently for 30 days, you will start to feel your self-esteem rise.

Start right now… list three things you have done well or right today so far:

1. _____

   _____

2. _____

   _____

3. _____

   _____

TECHNIQUE 5: BECOME AWARE OF YOUR SELF-TALK AND CHANGE IT!

Have you ever listened to your own self-talk? If anyone else had treated me the way I treated myself, or said the things to me that I did and said to myself, it would be considered emotional abuse!

Self-talk: the non-stop chatter that goes on in your head. My friend calls it "the Gremlins". We constantly engage in self-talk, and I'm wondering... what does yours say? "Who do you think you are?" "I'm too fat to wear that!" "That was stupid... what was I thinking?" "I'm a horrible human being!" "I'm worthless... I don't deserve... I'm nothing... no one will ever love me" and on and on. The non-stop chatter in our heads.

Here's the problem: your body will only do what your mind tells it to do. Your words, voice tone, inflection, body language, actions or inaction reflect what's going on inside of you!

When I was working at that ladies clothing store, as I went through my day it was constant for me: "I wasn't nice enough to that customer... I forgot to smile... I didn't fold those sweaters perfectly... I didn't sell enough... I don't know how to sweep a floor... that was wrong... I made a mistake... I'm worthless...". It was never ending. And at the end of every day, my friend would call and say: "How was your day today" and my response was the same every single day: "I'm pretty sure today is the day I get fired". Of course, I didn't get fired but my view of myself and the non-stop negative self-talk that supported that view kept me in such a state of worry and constant anxiety I felt like I was always walking around on eggshells! For the first 30 plus years of my life this is how I felt! It takes a lot of energy to walk around like that, not to mention the effect it has on our lives. We keep ourselves stuck, locked in this invisible emotional prison.

The previous two exercises are a way that we can start to turn this around and we need to, because whatever we place our attention on grows. If you focus on the negative it will grow and if you focus on the positive it will grow.

As you go through your day, listen to yourself. What do you say to yourself? What is your self-talk telling you? How is that manifesting in the outside world? Take a day or two and listen... maybe even write down the messages you give yourself. What are you telling yourself? How are you treating yourself?

You need to treat yourself the way you would treat someone you love. Would you ever say to someone you love "You never do anything right!" "You're a worthless human being!" "You're a really bad mother!" or any of the other things you tell yourself? I'm betting the answer is "NO! Of course not!" Then why do we feel it's OK to treat ourselves this way? Treat yourself the way you would treat someone you love. Speak to yourself the way you would speak to someone you love. When you catch yourself saying "You're worthless..." stop, stop right where you are and say something positive instead.

For example, one of my clients when having a bad day would turn to beating herself up: "I'm no good, I don't deserve any of this, I'm a rotten human being..." all because she was having a bad day. She learned to turn that around, and when the "gremlins" started she would stop them and say: "NO! I'm not a bad person, I am worthwhile, I am just having a bad day and it will pass" as a way to quiet her gremlins.

I still catch myself now. I'll be doing something... say writing a book... and the gremlins will come: "I'm so bad at this. I failed English, I can't write a book, no one will ever read this..." and on and on. But I catch myself, and it's not "I'm so bad at this" it's "Hey... I'm pretty good at this. This book sounds like me. And it's not about who or how many read the book – I'm writing it because I want to!"

The trick to this is you need to catch yourself when you're doing it. Sometimes it's hard and you need a "mirror". You need to enlist your friends or family, or even your co-workers. There is no shame in asking for help. Asking for help is not a sign of weakness, it's a sign of strength, so ask for help. Tell those closest to you that you need help in changing your self-talk and the next time they catch you berating yourself or saying something negative about yourself to stop you and ask you to rephrase it as something positive. Those closest to you will appreciate the opportunity to help you. Everyone likes to feel needed and important. You can give a powerful gift to someone by asking for their help.

Start the day by looking in the mirror and instead of finding everything wrong with yourself and your life, tell yourself something positive – "It's going to be a great day today!" or "You will go out and do your best today!" Because that's the bottom line… all we can do is our best. No one can ask more of us than that. The problem is that when we beat ourselves up so badly we are creating an outcome that is less than our best. So turn it around. From this moment forward when you catch yourself saying something negative to yourself STOP! Say something positive instead, no matter how small!

1. *What are the things you say to yourself? What do you KNOW you tell yourself on a regular basis?*
2. *How can you change your negative self-talk to positive self-talk? For every negative thing you know you say to yourself, how can you re-phrase that to be positive?*
3. *What one positive thing can you say to yourself every morning when you look in the mirror?*

Write down these positive phrases, this positive self-talk on sticky notes and stick them everywhere to remind you! Certainly place one on the bathroom mirror… the fridge door… your computer screen… the door of your cupboard. The more positive re-enforcement you can give yourself the better. You are trying to create new neural pathways, new ways of thinking. The old way of thinking is a habit and so you must think a new way as many times a day as possible to create the new habit!

SECRET #SIX:

Daily Activities for Developing Self-Esteem

*"It's not what you are that holds you back,
it's what you think you are not."*
Unknown

*"You, yourself, as much as anyone in the entire
Universe, deserve your love and affection."*
Buddha

The five techniques in the last chapter, if practised on a regular basis, will change your view of yourself. They'll change the way you think about yourself, even cause you to like, and dare I say... love yourself.

All this costs is time and effort, and not a lot of time at that – so those of you who are about to use the "I'm too busy" excuse, don't. The time investment is minimal. What it does take is mind space: effort, attention and energy. But think about all the effort, energy and attention you put into worrying about whether or not you are good enough, lovable enough or capable enough. The energy you spend in trying to hide who you really are so people won't "find out" or "see the real you". The effort you exert in trying to control people, places, things, situations and outcomes, and in trying to make sure you and everything else is perfect – well then, in comparison, this is nothing!

The best part about this is you can do this anywhere, anytime. You don't need to leave your house, you can do it at home while you're cooking dinner or doing chores, you can do it at work, you can do it while out shopping. I spent a fair bit of attention and energy focusing on this at work and it did not take away from my performance at all. As a matter of fact, the more attention I gave to developing my confidence and self-esteem, the more time I gave to focusing on the good things I did instead of beating myself up for the perceived bad things I did, the better my performance got and the quicker I could achieve promotions and pay raises. Because that's how it works – when you get better on the inside, the outside world responds positively, and almost immediately, and everything starts to change.

This is a journey, not a goal, and there are some things you can do that will change you instantly – for example, you may be feeling a little better about yourself, your life, your relationships just through reading this book. Sometimes it's a big relief to understand that you are not alone. Other things take constant attention and focus, and practice. For me, this practice is a forever one. While I'd love to tell you that I'm "fixed", this is not the case and I remember what it was like, how much I hated myself, my wrong thinking – so I don't dare stop! I know there are plenty of times where the old ways of thinking creep back in and I'm constantly tested. Take for example my family. My mother at 80 years of age is still a people-pleasing perfectionist. I still must be aware constantly of my own thoughts and remind myself of who I am *now* or I will revert to the old ways when in her presence.

Here's a quick and easy technique: Find a Role Model!

If confidence and healthy self-esteem is not modelled for you, in other words, if those you spent time with from an early age do not demonstrate healthy confidence and self-esteem, then you likely never learned what it was or what it looked like. We need role models!

Before anyone goes blaming their parents – parents do the best they can with what they have. No one sets out to intentionally harm their child, but sometimes it happens. We all do damage to our children. I think the goal is to keep it to a minimum. I don't blame my mother, but I had no idea about this self-esteem thing. I remember being in rehab and hearing this term for the first time. And then I remember seeing it and hearing about it everywhere! Until that point I was unaware of the concept and I certainly didn't know that I was lacking in it. And, I did not know that this was contributing to my situation and circumstances. I didn't know what I didn't know... and this is how learning occurs. In an instant, I moved to knowing that I didn't know and that opened the door to me learning about it. I became aware of it, in particular, my lack of it, it entered my radar screen and became part of what I paid attention to. This is what allowed me to learn – and it's never too late to learn!

Find a role model. Someone who has the confidence and self-esteem you desire for yourself. Observe them, hang out with them. Ask questions. That's what I did. I had a boss that just amazed me in the way she handled things. I remember her and her long-time boyfriend breaking up, and while she was understandably upset – she didn't fall apart. She didn't drink or take days off work or go shopping or engage in any other self-destructive activity. I was amazed! So I asked her about it: how did she feel, how was she coping with this? She was more than willing to share and I learned a lot about what confidence looks like. She was my emotional role-model for a long time and she never knew it.

It was the same for me when I came out of the fog of addiction – what did it look like to be a functioning human being? A woman? I didn't know, so I found someone I wanted to be like. She was elegant and graceful, everyone wanted to speak with her so I watched, and listened, and learned and it worked! Find someone you admire, observe, listen and ask questions. Allow them to be your model.

More techniques to try.

Fake It 'Till You Make It

As we discussed with self-fulfilling prophecies, we will always find proof of what we believe. If you believe your own negative self-talk then you will create the very thing you say you don't want. You, we, all of us are limited by what we believe is possible so stop the "I can't... it won't work... I'm not good enough... nothing good ever happens to me..." talk and any other self-limiting beliefs and open yourself to what IS possible. You don't know unless you try and you can create positive self-fulfilling prophecies as easily as you create negative ones!

You must change your beliefs about what is possible. "I'm never going to be able to love myself" will create that very thing. "I'm going to learn to practise loving myself" will also create that very thing. Read those two sentences again because it's a subtle difference linguistically between the two but a very big difference in the outcome. Your actions and behaviour follow your beliefs. It's simple. Change your beliefs and you will change the outcome. Start to believe you are worthwhile, that you are deserving, that you can be happy even if you don't really believe it deep down, tell yourself you do believe it. Tell yourself over and over again. It's called "Fake It 'Till You Make It". It's a real technique and it really works!

It works because your brain gives your body direction, so pretend you are lovable, you are kind, you are a good person, you deserve the good that life has to offer. Keep telling yourself this and watch what happens! You might be surprised! We often keep ourselves stuck because we don't believe things are possible… but again, the truth is – you don't know what's possible. Everything I said would never happen to me and things that I never ever in a million years thought were possible are, in fact, happening in my life right now. How did I get here? I faked it until it became a reality.

I behaved as if I had confidence, I behaved as if I was capable, I behaved as if I was a nice person, and soon, I wasn't "faking" it anymore. I believed it. And if I can do it… well then, what's your excuse?

You don't know what you're capable of or what is possible. You only know what you believe is possible and those beliefs came from forces outside yourself and were imprinted a long time ago and then you go on through your life believing that they are true. They are only true if you make them true! Create a new truth! That's what this work is about… opening to what's possible.

I'm feeling the need to refer to an example of a client who has now become my friend. When I met her, as talented and as good at her job as she was, she hated herself. She disliked people, she told herself she was no good at social interaction, she didn't know how to talk to people (talk about ridiculous negative self-talk – of course she knew how to talk to people! But she told herself she didn't and so she didn't), she told herself she was a horrible human being and had made catastrophic mistakes in her life (which I would like to point out – who hasn't?), she would never be happy and she didn't deserve to be happy.

She felt so badly about herself that she mostly worked from home to avoid people and only went into the office when she had to. I used to tell her: "Of course you can talk to people!" to which she would respond "No I can't! What would I say?" Because you see in her mind, she saw all the things she thought were wrong with her... from her perspective. She had a childhood that was fraught with difficult experiences with people, and she carried those with her and projected those on to others. She was sure that everyone else could see everything that she thought was wrong with her, every mistake she knew she had ever made, she believed other people knew that also. Of course, they didn't. How could they? Only we know what goes on inside of us... only we have our perception of our lives and events in our lives. (Do you ever talk to your siblings about your childhood only to find out they had a completely different experience than you did?) Even though it was 20 or more years ago, she still viewed the world through that lens.

She practised "faking it". She practised believing that she could talk to people, that people would be interested in what she had to say. And guess what? To her surprise... the behaviour she was "faking" very soon became her reality.

Fast forward two years after doing this work with me, and this is a direct quote from a recent email I received from her: "*...I don't know how to express how much stronger, happier, accepting of myself, at peace, content, grateful for my gifts... etc... I am.*"

So here is an incredibly intelligent, talented woman with a very important job who was sure that she would never find peace, happiness and contentment. But she did. Why? Because she trusted and she did the work. She tried. Because really – what do you have to lose? Fake it… just try. As I've said before, you can have your old life back anytime you want it!

This leads us to the next technique because it really ties into this one.

Stop Doing Other People's Thinking for Them

You can see it can't you? After the last two techniques? We're horrible for doing this! We do other people's thinking for them! We project what is in our mind out onto them! And it prevents us from getting what we want. It keeps us locked in that invisible prison!

I remember years ago, probably about three or four years into my journey to re-wire my brain, I discovered this. My self-esteem and confidence were rising and it came time for me to graduate from working at the ladies clothing store to a job in an office. But I had no recent experience, I had not worked on computers, it had been a long time since I had typed anything. My mind kept trying to tell me that this wouldn't work out, but I had learned that the answer is always "no" unless we ask the question, and I reasoned the worst thing that could happen is they say no. Still, to be on the safe side (and protect my self-esteem), I decided to start small and I applied at a Temporary Service Agency. I had worked in law offices and banks many years previously in England and so I thought this might be a good place to test the waters for going back into an office environment. I went in for "testing" at this Temp Agency and ended up getting taken on full time in the office. To this day I have to credit the Universe for this… I didn't apply for the job, I had no recent experience and yet they hired me anyway. I was excited and scared – surely this was a mistake? (Another example of how we can't possibly predict what the Universe has in store for us!)

About five or six months into the job I had been managing a large financial company account which was growing rapidly. We had hired and trained many people for this company and I was managing all of it, but the account didn't have an official "Account Manager" and it was getting so big they thought they needed one. The job posting went up in our office and in all the other offices in the area for a "Senior Account Manager". The job posting listed all the things I was currently managing on the account… the job was perfect for me! Except for one thing… they were looking for a "Senior" Account Manager and I had only been at this job for a few months. There were many "senior" people in my office as well as the offices in the surrounding area and I (in my estimation) was not one of them. I really wanted this job – I had been doing it and I felt I was doing it pretty well. I wanted to apply… I really did… but my self-talk said something different: "You won't get the job, you're not "senior" enough". "If you apply for the job they will say no and then it will be uncomfortable. You don't want to put the District Manager in a position where she has to say no and then she'll feel bad!" So I didn't apply. Why? Because I was doing my District Manager's thinking for her. I thought she would say no because I didn't have enough experience. So rather than putting her in a bad position, I didn't apply.

The job posting stayed up a month. And every once in a while I would casually ask my manager if they had found anyone yet. The answer was always "No, not yet." I *really* wanted this job… but in my mind it would have been foolish to apply because I didn't have the skills and experience they were looking for and the answer would be no. But what have I said about projecting our view of the world onto others? I was stopping myself from applying for the job by doing my District Manager's thinking for her.

Then came the very last day for the posting. It closed for applications at 5:00 p.m. – the office closing time. The night before I remember sitting on my bed and thinking "I really want that job… I really want to apply for that job" and all I can tell you is that my entire body was consumed with waves of goosebumps while I was thinking this. My thinking went from "I really want that job" to "I'm going to apply for that job" while sitting on my bed that night. Because when I thought about applying for the job the wave of goosebumps would come… I had felt this before and it seemed to me it was my sign that the decision was right.

The next day I went into work with the intention of applying for the job. My District Manager happened to be working from our office that day. All day I wandered by the posting re-reading it, wanting to apply for the job, but that word "Senior" kept getting in the way. "Maybe I was wrong... I had no experience... it was just a fluke that I even got hired in this office and one day they would figure out that I was a low-life and didn't deserve to be here..." kept running through my mind. All day I was in turmoil – wanting the job and yet convinced I wouldn't be hired.

Now it was 4:50 p.m. The office and the job posting was closing in 10 minutes. I was cleaning up my desk, and across from me my Manager was cleaning up some files. Again, I casually asked: "So, have they found anyone for the Senior Account Manager position?" "No, not yet" was the response from my Manager. Silence followed. And now it was 4:58 and I looked up at my Manager and out of nowhere came the words: "I should really apply for that job shouldn't I?" She looked me straight in the eyes and said: "Yes. You really should."

Off I went visibly shaking into the District Manager's office. After asking permission to enter (yeah, I know – but if it is possible to have less than zero confidence and self-esteem that's what I had), I sat down in the chair in front of her desk, hands clasped in my lap, eyes looking downward. "Judi... uh... um..." Good start! "Uh... I... uh... I would really like to apply for the Account Manager position (I couldn't bring myself to say the word "Senior"), I know I don't have a lot of experience but I have a relationship with them, I know the account, the General Manager and I have become quite good friends and I really think I could do a good job." And then I took a deep breath and looked up. Judi sat back in her chair visibly relieved and said: "Well, thank God! I was starting to get worried!" I looked at her, confused. "We wrote the job posting for you! It's your job! We didn't know what to do when you didn't apply... we thought you didn't want it!"

So... lesson learned. Do not do other people's thinking for them! You have no idea what is in their mind, you have no idea how they see you, your skills, your talents and worth. You only know what you think and as we've discussed... that's probably wrong!

And yet, how often do we do this? We stop ourselves from asking for things because we're sure the answer will be "no". Well the answer is always going to be "no" unless you ask the question!

Stop and think: how many times today have you done someone else's thinking for them? "I should call my friend... oh... she's probably busy at work and I don't want to bother her so I won't call...". "I'd really like to go out to see a movie this weekend but everyone is probably busy. They all have families and things to do. I'll just stay here at home and watch a movie on TV." "I should ask for a raise or promotion... but why bother... I won't get it anyway." Talk about keeping ourselves locked in an invisible prison!

- *Notice today... how many times have you done someone else's thinking for them?*
- *How many times have you predicted an outcome and prevented yourself from doing something because of it?*
- *How many times do you think this "prophesising" stands in your way?*
- *What can you do to stop the next time you catch yourself?*

Stop Measuring Your Insides Against Everyone Else's Outsides!

Have you ever noticed that you do this? I'm not sure if men do it but I know women certainly do! **We measure our insides against everyone else's outsides.** These negative messages we carry around about ourselves that guide our thoughts, actions, and choices. We feel less than, not good enough, unlovable, incapable. Our lives are falling apart, we're unhappy, our relationships aren't what we had hoped for... and then when we encounter someone who appears happy and successful on the outside, and who tells us how wonderful their life is, we feel somehow "less than" – which only serves to support our negative beliefs about ourselves. The truth is, we don't really know what's going on with the other person on the inside; we're only looking at the outside and measuring our inside thoughts and feelings against the other person's outside appearance. It's like comparing an orchid and a brick wall. The two are very different.

Whatever another person's appearances, we must realise that we cannot accurately guess what's going on inside. There is no point in comparing our happiness factor with theirs because you really don't know!

Just look at Hollywood starlets… they appear to have everything! Money, beautiful houses, they themselves are beautiful in appearance, they wear stunning clothes and go to fancy parties and we think how perfect their lives are. Well, if their lives are so perfect, how do you reconcile the amount of substance abuse, anorexia, low self-esteem and destructive tendencies among these very same "beautiful" people?

You cannot measure how you feel on this inside against how others look on the outside. It's an unfair comparison. I know myself, I used to decorate my outside in perfectly painted nails, a nice suit and high heels, all to hide the fact that I felt like I didn't measure up on the inside. If anyone were comparing themselves to me they would have thought I looked like I had it all – because I did look like I had it all and it was a strategy to throw people off so they wouldn't see the mess I was inside.

Everyone has problems, no matter how they look on the outside. Money does not make you happy, it just makes life a little more comfortable. Only you can make you happy and it doesn't come from what you own or what you look like on the outside. Happiness comes from within. It comes from being comfortable in who you are. I always say that happiness is wanting what you have. Trying to buy things to make you happy or keep up with your friends or colleagues doesn't work. It may make you happy temporarily… but it also wears off and you have to buy more things to get that happiness high again. So stop comparing your insides to other people's outsides. Know that everyone has their version of problems, some big, some little, but problems nonetheless and the feelings we have are all the same.

- Take a few minutes and think about it…
- *Who do you compare yourself to?*
- *Do you think their insides match their outsides or is it possible they have problems too?*
- *What can you do to remember to stop comparing your inside to others' outside?*

Here's my favourite quote and it comes from a t-shirt (I own six of them so I will never forget…): *"Happiness is found when you stop comparing yourself to other people and believe in yourself."*

Talk About It – Bring It Out into The Light

This is a powerful technique and a very important one. Whatever it is you are suffering with… whatever wrong you think you have done or has been done to you, you can't keep it locked inside. You must talk about it… bring it out into the light.

Emotions are a very powerful thing. They are not logical, they are messy, you can't avoid them or shut them down – but you can ignore them and suppress them. There is, however, a danger in doing that: emotions trigger a chemical release in the brain, and negative emotions like fear, anxiety, negativity, and frustration cause chemical reactions in your body that are very different from the chemicals released when you feel positive emotions like being loved, content, happy and accepted.

Emotions are signals as to what is going on in us, and when we ignore or avoid negative emotions… say for example feeling angry or hurt by someone, or feeling not important, not loved, or worthless, or when we stuff them down, refuse to feel them and therefore can't release them, we are setting ourselves up for some serious problems. Emotions – felt or ignored – control your thinking, behaviour and actions. When we don't feel, and release them, they don't go away. Oh no… instead, they bury themselves within our bodies and/or minds and can cause serious illnesses like cancer, arthritis and many types of chronic illness. Personally, lack of challenge causes depression in me. As soon as I can recognise it… feel it and bring it out into my consciousness, I can fix it and the depression goes away. And being married to a police officer, which, let's face it, is a profession skilled at compartmentalising and burying their emotions (it seems to me that it's a coping technique because what they see every day is more than a person should have to bear), I can't help but wonder if all the years of locking away the unpleasant emotions isn't what causes all the heart disease among them. Just my opinion of course, but still… you have to wonder.

As long as you keep these emotions and feelings locked up, they continue to have power over you. They are still there operating in the background. Driving our thoughts, behaviours, actions and ideas… driving our self-talk, causing us to do others' thinking for them, teaching other people how to treat us… we don't intentionally do this, but emotions are a powerful thing and they guide our actions and decisions. As long as they are still down there, they have the power to guide our life.

The only way to take the power away from them is to bring them out and talk about them. Once you talk about them you shine a light on them and when they are out in the light they lose the power to control you. It's very powerful!

For most of us, these feelings and emotions we keep hidden are deeply rooted and painful in some way. And we are sure that if other people find out then something horrible will happen. But here's the thing, I've said it before… we all feel this way. We all have some trauma, some secrets that we're sure make us bad people. It's only by sharing those, by seeing the reaction of the person you are telling, by sharing and being accepted and loved anyway that we can prove to ourselves that we are worthwhile. As long as we keep this stuff locked up we perpetuate the "worthless, not good enough, unlovable, incapable" self-view and self-talk. And that's not how you develop self-esteem!

Whatever it is, you must talk about it! To a stranger, a therapist, a friend, someone you trust, it doesn't matter… but you must talk about it. I remember the youngest step-son of a friend of mine whose biological mother committed suicide. He kept these feelings of anger at her for leaving him, his guilt for feeling this way, his fear that he would end up like his mother, his grief over her death locked up so deep inside that it eventually caused depression in him. It was only when he could bring himself to talk about these things, how they made him feel, what he was afraid of, it was only then that he could begin to accept what had happened.

He needed to see that just because he felt this way didn't make it true… he wasn't a bad person because he was angry at his mother, he wasn't a bad person because he didn't think he cried enough or grieved her death properly. Just because this happened to his mother does not mean it will happen to him. Once he could get this out, he could see the feelings and the fear for what they were – human. Once he could get these out they no longer had power over him, they no longer dictated his feelings about himself, and his depression cleared itself up. This is the power of bringing it to the light.

And no, this is not easy. Some of the "confessions" I have heard are clearly very painful for the person telling me. But there is not one thing that I have heard that makes someone a bad person. They just make them human beings doing the best they can with what they have at the time. And it's the same for you!

All the people I have worked with over the years, upon using this technique and doing one of the most difficult things imaginable: talking about their feelings, about themselves and the perceived wrongs they have done in their lives, have the same experience afterward – relief. They feel (as I did) like a giant weight had been lifted off their shoulders, they felt free. One more bar of that invisible prison disintegrated.

The only reason I know this is because for years I made up a "back-story" about who I was and where I had come from. I was so terrified that if I told people the truth they would run away or throw rotten fruit at me (ridiculous I know but feelings are rarely logical and when we keep them locked up they grow and grow and become all consuming!). I hid behind clothes and jewellery, I lied about my past, all so that people wouldn't find out the truth. The few people I did tell were amazed at how I was still alive, some wanted to know more, but then I could justify that as they really didn't understand what a *horrible person* I truly was. And this went on for years.

And then I wrote the book *An Invisible Prison*, and before it was published I had to go to all my world-class clients, and friends and colleagues and tell them this story about who I really was (because of course, I had been doing their thinking for them and I didn't want them to suddenly not speak to me anymore or fire me). Well, imagine my surprise when ALL of them said: "Wow! I had no idea... you are amazing" or variations of that. I never lost a single client or a single friend by telling them this (what in my mind was a) horrible truth. And all those years I had spent lying and hiding and allowing this fear to grow and govern everything I did and everything I said... and for what? It was wasted energy.

- *What are you hiding? What do you need to talk about and bring to the light?*
- *What is the reaction you are afraid of? What do you think the other person, when you share, will say/do?*
- *Do you have any evidence that these beliefs are true? (The answer is no, you don't have any proof.)*
- *Who can you talk to about this? Who can you share these deep feelings with? Who is "safe" for you?*
- *When will you do this?*

Once you have shared with someone, take a moment and write down their reaction. I'm asking you to do this so you can go back to remind yourself that the fear of what people will think resides only in your head – you are doing other people's thinking for them! Which brings us to the subject of fear...

Release Yourself from Fear

There are acronyms about fear: False Evidence About Reality, and False Evidence Appearing Real. I like them both because they are true. There is a difference between a healthy fear and an unhealthy one. The problem is, we respond to all fear the same – as if it's real – and we allow it to stop us from moving forward. Fear keeps us locked in our invisible prison.

We are human, and fear is a normal part of life. The greatest of human fears is not public speaking, it's fear of the unknown. Think about it... isn't fear what stops you from making the changes you want in your life? You don't like your job so you think about quitting – and then fear takes over. "But what if I can't find another job?", "I'm too old, no one will hire me", "What if I can't find a job that pays as well as this one?" And we end up buying into the "what ifs", the fear, and prevent ourselves from finding a new job that will likely make us happier.

I had a client who was so frustrating for me... she was miserable at her job. Bored, lacking challenge, de-motivated. She didn't want to go to work, she didn't want to talk to her colleagues, it took her so much time and energy just to do her job she was exhausted all the time! In one of our sessions I asked her: "If you are so unhappy at work, why do you stay? Why don't you start looking for another job?" I'm sure by now you can guess her answer. There was a list a mile long of reasons she told herself why she couldn't quit and find another job: no other company would pay as well, there were no other companies that would hire for her position as close to her house, she had already spent over 20 years at this company, she'd be compromising her pension... and the list went on and on.

This is a logical, rational, highly intelligent woman who was compromising her health, happiness and emotional well-being for the sake of money. How is that logical? And yet, these were the stories she told herself. She was afraid. Paralysed by the fear that she wouldn't get another job, and that even if she did, she might not find one she was happy at. Are any of these fears real? I don't know... and neither will you unless you try.

And yet this is what we do... we create these imaginary scenarios in our minds and then operate on the basis that they are real when the truth is – you don't know! Fear is not fact. It is false evidence... evidence that resides in your mind only, and not necessarily out in the real world.

Now, I'm not saying that some fears don't come true. Of course they do. But they never come true the exact way we think they will. My client did not want to leave her job because she was afraid... but she also believed there was nothing else she could do in her own company. She believed she was stuck where she was. After much convincing by me to test the water, to just *try* to see what else there was within her own organisation that she might be interested in, she found something. Now she is doing a completely different job than she was doing when I met her, she has developed an entirely new skill set that she loves, she loves her job again and best of all, she is no longer unhappy and depressed. She now gets upset if she CAN'T go in to work!

Fear. False evidence. I learned many powerful lessons when my father died. I've already shared the one around conditioning and I learned a powerful lesson about fear as well.

My father was incredibly talented. But he was terrified. He was so afraid that "there would never be enough" (an imprint from living in Britain during World War II), so afraid to take a risk that he never did anything with his talent. He would invent things for his company that saved them thousands of pounds and never got any credit for it. He had money… but he never travelled – he was afraid. I used to try to get him to go on Seniors' vacations. To travel and do the things he always dreamed of, but he always had the same excuse: he couldn't afford it. Not knowing his financial situation while he was alive I couldn't argue. But I'll tell you I was very angry after he died and I found out he DID have the money… he was just afraid.

I made my mind up right then I would not live my life based on fear. I would acknowledge the fear (which for me shows up in my stomach), I would feel it, and if it felt like an unhealthy fear then damn it, I was going to do the thing anyway! Like applying for that job as the Senior Account Manager. I was terrified… terrified I wasn't good enough. But I did it anyway. My father's fear taught me an important lesson: I do not want to get to the end of my life and say "I wish I had done…" whatever it is I'm afraid to do.

I'm afraid all the time. There was a time when I was terrified of everything – of people, of not being in control, of not being perfect (I'm exhausted thinking about that). Now, after doing the work I'm suggesting you do, I'm not afraid of people anymore, it's also caused me to not need to be in control all the time because I trust my ability to manage whatever comes my way and, thanks to the self-esteem and confidence, I know I'm not perfect and I don't care. As long as I do my best. But I still get afraid… every time I go and work with a new company, or a new group. I'm afraid writing this book... what if no one reads it? What if no one likes it? But I'm not allowing this fear to stop me. I'm doing it anyway.

I do all kinds of things that would scare most people. I remember the first time I went to work in Saudi Arabia I was terrified! All the research I had done hadn't done me a bit of good... everything I read was wrong and, as it turned out, all my fears were unfounded – false evidence that in this case appeared real because of the internet! You can be afraid, you just can't let it stop you.

People always tell me I have a lot of courage, and I do. I agree. But only because I have an enormous amount of fear! You can't have courage without fear. Courage is feeling the fear but not letting it stop you. Instead of seeing fear as something that prevents you from moving ahead, how about re-framing it and turning it into a positive self-fulfilling prophecy? How about FEAR standing for Face Everything And Rise? Sounds much better doesn't it?

Here are some tips for managing fear:

1. Pay attention to how or where your fear shows up – in your stomach? Shoulders? Head? What does it feel like?

2. When you feel it, don't immediately see it as a sign that something is wrong. It's not wrong, it's just different, so stop and ask yourself if it's a real fear – a healthy one? For example, I fear that if I drink alcohol I might very well end up right back where I was. A healthy fear for me. If you're overweight you might fear that if you don't lose weight you might end up with health problems and possibly death. A healthy fear.

Or is it an unhealthy fear? If I ask for a raise I will get turned down. Unhealthy. You don't know unless you ask. If I leave my relationship I will never find another one. Unhealthy. You don't know that to be true. If I confront my mother she won't love me anymore. Unhealthy. You don't know. I think you get the idea.

I got in the habit of feeling the football in my stomach and asking myself: "Is anyone going to die if I do this? Am I going to die if I do this?"

Extreme maybe, but that's what worked for me. And if the answer was "no", then I went ahead and did whatever I was afraid to do. And just so you know... it's never turned out badly. It hasn't always turned out perfectly but it's always ended up representing growth on my part.

3. Start small. Do one thing today that makes you uncomfortable. Take a different way to work. Drive instead of taking public transport or vice-versa. Go to a new restaurant or go to a different grocery store for shopping – that's enough to test anyone's courage! It's very frustrating when you don't know where things are!

4. Make a habit of stepping outside of your comfort zone. It's called a comfort zone because that's where you're comfortable. But if you're always comfortable you're not stretching yourself. You're not growing, you're not changing, you're not learning. You are staying still. If you do what you've always done you will get what you've always got. Do something differently. That's how you move forward.

5. Become comfortable with the discomfort. The more comfortable you become taking risks, being uncomfortable, the easier it becomes. Remember, the things you want aren't going to come to you unless you step out into the unknown first. So, become comfortable with the unknown. What's out there might surprise you.

6. Take one action, any action, toward what it is you want. Try one technique of the many listed in this book. Just one. The Universe always rewards action. Do one thing differently today and it will change your tomorrow. Because that's how it works.

7. You are in control of you! Your actions, thoughts, and beliefs will either create positive outcomes or negative outcomes. It all starts with you. Any outcome can be positive or negative depending on how you look at it.

Fear is a powerful motivator... use it for good instead of letting it paralyse you!

And don't forget:

- *Who you are is good enough. Self-esteem is your power base. Fear becomes less daunting when you trust and believe in yourself.*
- *Stay in the present. Dwelling on the past keeps you stuck there. Worrying about the future is wasted energy because you don't know what the future holds. All you have is today. Do something different today, right now.*
- *Recognise you have choices. It's all about choices. We can choose at any given time how and what to think, how to behave, what to do. You are the only thing you can control... only you can choose how to feel about yourself, how to live your life, and how happy to be.*
  Choose happy.

Take a few moments and reflect on your own circumstances...

- *What are you afraid of?*
- *What steps can you take to test this fear?*
- *What small steps can you take to begin to manage this fear and prove it wrong?*
- *What are you willing to do to step out of your comfort zone today?*

PART TWO:
Harness the Power of the Universe and Set Yourself Free

"Always remember the primary purpose of your life is living in tune with your energy pattern, find the true expression for the energy and go with the flow!"
Ramana Pemmaraju

SECRET #SEVEN:

The Science of the Universe

"you are That" (tat tvam asi)
The Upanishads

*"The cosmos is within us. We are made of star-stuff.
We are a way for the universe to know itself."*
Carl Sagan

I know the techniques for re-wiring your brain work – I've done it. I'm living proof. People always ask me how I got from where I was – homeless, addicted and abused – to where I am today, and the techniques I have shared in the last two chapters are part of it. But there is another piece to this as well.

I spent years studying the science of the mind and of human interaction in order to re-learn everything about being a functioning human being. But after about 10 years or so I got stuck. I hit a wall... I reached the limits of my ability to help myself. I knew there was something more that I was missing. I knew there was a next step but I didn't know what it was. Psychology hadn't answered all my questions about how and why my life had turned out the way it did and so I turned to Spirituality.

Not being raised in a religious or spiritual household this was a stretch for me but the pain of my existence... the depression I was feeling... the misery I was experiencing was enough to allow me to start to explore. And this is one of the keys we will explore in Chapter 9: when the pain of your existence outweighs the fear of change, you will change. For me, there was nothing wrong with my life. I had created a wonderful career that was perfect for who I am, designing and facilitating workshops for major corporations. I was busy, I had no financial problems, a great husband, two step-children who were wonderful, a beautiful house… and yet I was miserable. And it made me feel guilty, and generally very bad about myself. I also knew that my emotional sobriety was first and foremost. I knew that if I didn't look after my emotional self then everything else would fall apart because, let's face it, I have a history of self-destructive tendencies.

In one of those divinely orchestrated moments (which this chapter is about) I came across a teacher – a spiritual teacher – and this led me to another 10 years of study about Spirituality. I studied with two teachers over the 10 years, both brilliant and powerful. One was a PhD and one an MD – Doctor Deepak Chopra, and it was he who introduced me to the world of Quantum Physics and the science behind Spirituality, a study which I continue today.

This is an important study for me as it explains the science of miracles and why I don't believe in luck. Before we get to the spiritual principles though, I want to tell you the story of why I have no choice but to believe in a power greater than myself, and the science that goes with that. So for all of you sceptics… this one's for you!

A Power Greater Than Ourselves

In the last two years of my drinking I was a mess – incapable of working, of carrying on a conversation, of even functioning day-to-day. I looked in the mirror and all I saw were all the horrible things I had done in the past, I couldn't see a future and I didn't want to live. I spent two years actively trying to kill myself through substance abuse and it NEVER worked. No matter how much or how many various substances I put in my body I would wake up the next morning – disappointed and seriously ill. I would lie on the sofa in my father's apartment and talk to the ceiling… I didn't know who I was talking to, I don't even think I thought about it at the time, but I used to look up at the ceiling and say: "Please… please…

just let me die. Why won't you let me die? Please... please... just let me get hit by a bus on my way to the off-licence. No one will care. Everyone expects it anyway... please, please... just let me die."

The ceiling did not listen.

Fast forward two years or so. I have told you the story of my quitting my job in a drunken stupor; well it was that next morning that I woke up, opened a warm beer, took two sips and then poured it down the sink. It was the last time I took a drink (I had quit drugs years before; alcohol was always my drug of choice). People always ask me: "What was the turning point?" There was no turning point, there was no magic situation or words that caused me to stop. I know what I believe happened and that is divine intervention – even though I wasn't aware of it at the time.

I had major health problems, I had bad headaches, PMS, wicked mood swings, trouble breathing... I was a physical mess and I knew that no doctor would touch me while I was still drinking. So I decided that stopping was the right thing to do. I also knew I needed help and I knew that Alcoholics Anonymous advertised in the newspaper so I dragged my hungover, sweating, throwing up every 15 minutes self to the corner shop to buy a paper. Why didn't I reach for the phone book, you ask? Well... therein lies the point in this chapter. I don't know. I do know that from the minute I poured that beer down the sink I was no longer in control.

There was no AA advertisement in the newspaper but there was an ad for "Phoenix House" (the metaphor here is just too profound to not mention). The ad spoke to me so I called the number and set up an appointment for the following day. The following day came, I got on the bus, went into town, found the address and commenced pacing back and forth outside. What if I wasn't good enough? What if they couldn't help me? What if I got the time wrong? What if, what if, what if... and then I saw a man who looked homeless walking toward me with a tray of coffee and big toothless grin. "Hi!" he said. "Are you coming in?" and he held the door open for me, coffee in one hand, door in the other. Well, if nothing else I was certainly raised to not upset other people so of course I said

"Yes" and went through the door. He asked why I was there and I told him I had an appointment with a counsellor. "Oh," he said, "you must be seeing Lynne" and called up the stairs. Moments later this big, burly tattooed man in a short-sleeved yellow shirt came walking down the stairs. Lynne turned out to be Lin. Short for Linwood. He was a recovering drug addict and ex-biker and he was to be my counsellor.

I've paused here to make a point... if Lin had been Lynne would this ever have worked? I don't think so. Because if Lynne had been a woman, I would never have felt good enough to be in her presence let alone speak to her. But Lin – a man who understood my past – I could talk to him, and I did.

I ended up in rehab in California. And one of the first things they told me is that to recover you must believe in "a power greater than yourself". I can't even describe my disappointment – something greater than myself? Something greater than a human being? There was nothing greater than a human being. We were top of the food chain. God? Were they talking about God? You can't see God. There is no proof of God. I knew I was in trouble because not only didn't I believe in God, I didn't understand the concept. I questioned... "a power greater than ourselves... I don't understand... what are you asking me to believe in?"

"It doesn't matter" was the answer, "it can be a table, a chair, a doorknob, but you have to believe that a power greater than yourself can restore you to sanity."

A doorknob? Seriously? I wondered what I had got myself into... were these all just Californian New Age hippies?

But this was my last chance, it was this or death, so I tried... I asked my fellow inmates... most believed in God but I knew nothing of this. I wasn't raised that way. Two weeks into the program and I was sure it wasn't going to work for me. These were all "normal" people with lives and jobs and families. They just happened to drink too much or like drugs too much. And then there was me... lowlife, worthless, ex-biker chick, ex-homeless person. I found it difficult to even speak to anyone, and to make matters worse they sent us to meetings... and since I was the only female with 11 males in the rehab facility, they drove me to women's meetings!

These women would talk about hiding wine in the back of the toilet and in the washing machine. They talked about embarrassing their husbands and children. And then there was me. I knew nothing about any of this... this didn't even seem like a problem to me, so once again it became evident to me that I didn't fit in and this wasn't going to work. I was convinced that if I opened my mouth to speak they would see me for the worthless human being I was and kick me out so no, I would not speak.

After two very frustrating weeks of trying to understand this concept of a "higher power", of listening to these good people talk about problems that I didn't understand, I decided this wasn't going to work and I should just leave. Here it was, my last chance, and I didn't even fit in here. I decided to escape, hitchhike back across the country and go back to the gang. I'd probably get killed but... isn't that what I had been hoping for for years anyway? And I decided the next time they drove me to a women's meeting would be an opportune time. So, after crying through the next women's meeting, comfortable that I had given sobriety my best shot, I went out to get my ride back to the rehab and the van wasn't there! This was my chance to escape! I starting walking down the street to the main road to hitchhike but halfway there the van pulled up and back to the rehab I went.

I couldn't stop crying... I had tried... I had really tried. We went to a meeting across the street at the main hospital that night and my rehab friend, the bank manager, escorted me to the meeting. We took our tickets for the draw (they always had a draw for a prize at the end of every meeting) and I went to the very back corner of the room and found a seat, my escort beside me. I cried through the entire meeting. I have no idea who spoke or what was said I was so lost in my own thoughts of escaping and what I considered to be the end of my life.

It was going to be the end of my life – but not in the way that I thought.

At the very end of the meeting they held the draw for the winning ticket. I wasn't paying attention because I never win anything, so imagine my surprise when my escort was tugging on my shirt sleeve, saying: "Sue... Sue... you won! You won! Go and get your prize!" Well now I wasn't just crying I was sobbing... the kind where you are physically heaving and unable to breathe... and I went up, grabbed the book I had won (it was *The Big Book* of Alcoholics Anonymous and I still have it) and took off running out the door... down the corridor... across the street... and into my room. Sobbing the entire way, clutching the book to my chest, and I stood there, alone, in my room, book clutched to my chest, and once again I looked at the ceiling... because the moment wasn't lost on me.

I was leaving because this wasn't going to work for me, and right after I made that decision I had won this book. I had never won anything in my life... and yet I won this book. It was a sign and I knew it, so once again I looked to the ceiling – "You're not going to let me leave even if I want to, are you?" I asked. And I heard a voice... "No Sue, we're not".

The only way I can describe what happened next is that it was like what they say happens when you die... my life, all the bad things, all the times I should have died and didn't, flashed before my eyes in a matter of seconds and, instinctively, I understood. I went to sleep that night knowing that "they" had saved me for a reason, "they" had given me this life for a reason, I was getting a second chance. I slept that night like I had never slept before. And when I awoke... the world was different and I was different. I understood what a "higher power" meant. I understood that I had been given my life for a reason. I didn't know by whom but that didn't matter... all that mattered was that I didn't waste it. I was given this life, these experiences, for a purpose and I had to make them count. I decided that morning that the purpose of my life was to live up to my full potential... whatever that was. And I decided I would pay "them" back... I would somehow find a way to use my experiences to help others, to touch people in a positive way every single day to pay back this second chance. It's the reason I do what I do. It's why I wrote this book.

Something greater than myself was at work here. Something greater than myself orchestrated my finding the Phoenix House, carried me through that next week – that I have almost no memory of – something greater than myself tapped me on the shoulder that morning and said "OK, enough now." Something greater than myself has orchestrated my life every step of the way and continues to do so. Of that I'm convinced. I believe in a power greater than myself because I feel that, in my life, there is too much evidence of this fact to ignore.

The Miracle of the Mind and Body

It took me 10 years or so of re-wiring my brain using psychological science before I hit that wall of "Ok, now what?" I knew there was something more that I was to do… but I didn't know how to find it so I turned to Spirituality to understand the meaning of my life. And I found it… in spiritual principles which I will talk about in the next chapters, and I found what I needed in the form of "proof" of this power which I just simply call The Universe – in Quantum Physics. And that's why I'm telling you all this.

Miracles have happened in my life and they are happening and will continue to happen in yours if you pay attention. There is no such thing as luck in my opinion. It's cosmic forces at work. The intelligence of the Universe to organise itself.

Quantum Physics helped me understand this… as much as any human can I suppose.

Have *you* ever stopped to think about the miracle of how your body works? How does your body heal itself? How does it know to keep breathing? The intelligence in your body to know when something is wrong and send the signals that send the appropriate cells or antibodies to heal it is beyond comprehension. And our mind… how does this powerful computer work? How does it know? Why are we born able to read facial expressions and voice tone and inflection? How does a baby animal come out of the womb and instantly start to walk? How does all this work? Medical science doesn't really know. The amount they know is far smaller than the amount they don't know.

Debates among scientists are going on all the time as to how memory is formed, where it is stored, how muscle memory works, how our bodies heal themselves. The intelligence in your body is amazing... the brain... the mind... the ability we have to think... where does a thought come from? No one knows. How do these thoughts get translated into words? And consciousness... what is it? Where does it come from? Scientists still argue about consciousness and what it is and where it is located. There are so many mysteries that science is trying to solve.

We always call the ground we walk on solid. But is it really? If it's so solid, then why do we have ground penetrating radar? Why can we see through something that is supposedly solid? The colour purple... is it really purple? I would argue that it's only purple because when light waves reflect off the object you are looking at they hit the retina in the back of your eye, and contained in this retina are tiny cells called cones. These cones are not all the same, so the light waves stimulate the cones to varying degrees and a signal is sent along the optic nerve to the visual cortex of your brain which processes the information and returns with a colour: purple. But it's only purple because that's the name we have arbitrarily hung on this stimulation of the cones and associated signal. So, is it really purple? Or is it only purple because we say it's purple?

Why am I telling you all of this? Because we operate based on what we know, and we call what we know "facts". But most of the "facts" that we know aren't really facts. It is our reality, which is nothing more than our subjective perception. The ground is not solid, it's made up of particles, very tightly knit particles but particles nonetheless. Reality as we experience it is not so much "real" as it is our subjective interpretation of what we are experiencing. So, to explain how these miracles work, I must bring in Quantum Physics.

Some of you are probably cringing at this point – Quantum Physics – really? Yes, really. But I'm not going to give you a big sciency lecture. Just enough to allow you to see how it's possible that a power greater than ourselves exists, and exists within us! And how this is tied to some of the things we have already explored, like energy and the possibility of miracles. And please remember, I am not a physicist, and I'm certainly no expert on this. I'm just someone who likes to know the *why* behind things. Like *why* I didn't die when I should have. *Why* my life has been the way it is. Quantum Physics has helped me put some science to this and helped me to answer *why* in a way that satisfies my curiosity. For now.

You Are the Universe and the Universe is You

Quantum Physics, or quantum mechanics, concerns itself with two things: waves and sub-atomic particles. Sometimes a particle can act like a wave and sometimes a wave can act like a particle. Confusing isn't it? Here's what you need to know and it's a chicken and egg thing so I don't know which one really comes first, only that in my opinion both are important to our purpose here.

There is a field of study (I'm careful not to call it a fact because scientists don't really know; they are theorising based on current research) around what is called Zero Point. Zero Point is an unlimited energy source which is the substance and energetic force behind all things created in the Universe. It's the reservoir, it holds all the energy from which everything is created. It's called the Zero Point Field. Everything comes from here (according to current thinking).

This energy connects everything in the Universe to everything else. Everything, including us, no matter how big or small, is energy interacting with the Zero Point Field. These quantum waves (quantum meaning the smallest of the small) also encode information. Think about how your cell phone works, or a television or Satellite Navigation System – the information is travelling through energy, through waves from one place to another. Everything is made up of energy... and particles. Sub-atomic particles that are so small that you can't see them. Even science doesn't have a powerful enough microscope so see these sub-atomic particles.

The theory is that when these particles come together they form masses. Early in the formation of the Universe, these masses became stars and planets, and eventually they evolved into some pretty sophisticated masses like animals, trees, flowers and plants which have the intelligence to know when to grow and bloom, and the most sophisticated of all... these particles formed human beings. And as the particles move and shift they create waves, or energy. All of us, everything in this Universe, is the same... made of the same particles. We are connected... we are the Universe and the Universe is us. We are the Universe in human form. As is written in The Upanishads *"you are That" (tat tvam asi)*.

So what does this mean? It means that you (a big bundle of atoms and sub-atomic particles that are always moving and shifting) are emitting energy. And remember what I said? Whatever you put out there is what you will get back. Because you are emitting energy, the mass of particles which is you is vibrating and emitting that vibration out into the world. And your vibration will either attract or repel others depending on their vibration. Whenever you are around someone who is negative or angry, they never need to say a word... you can feel it! You can feel their vibration, their energy. We are like big radio antennas... always emitting and receiving waves of energy.

It also means that because we are the Universe and the Universe is us, we have access to this infinite field of knowledge and wisdom. We are a creation of the Universe, and all we have to do is look around to see the intelligence of the Universe, and since we are the Universe and the Universe is us, that same intelligence lies within us. We have access to it. Do I believe that I heard the "voice of God" in that hospital room in rehab? No. I heard a voice alright but I believe that voice came from inside me. The infinite intelligence that resides in each of us. It was my true self, my higher self if you will, the one who knows what my path is, which direction I should go. The part of me that has the power to heal itself, that knows the answer to my life's dilemmas. The small voice inside that says: "Go this way", or in my case "OK, it's time to stop". It is the Universe inside me, inside all of us, that knows the truth.

Surrendering to the Flow

We are one with the Universe. We are made of the same stuff. We emit light just as a star emits light. But, as humans, we have an ego. This is the thing that keeps us separate, it makes us individual, it lets us know that we are not the next person... that we are a separate person. And it gets in the way. Our ego's job is to get us through life safely. Our logical rational mind, our ego, wants to control, wants to orchestrate and plan and set goals and carry out our lives the way *WE* think they are supposed to go because it seeks pleasure and avoids pain. And in doing so, we create situations and circumstances for ourselves that are not in keeping with who we really are. This is what causes us unhappiness, pain, and depression. This is how we create our invisible prison.

The Universe is infinitely intelligent – once again you just have to think about your body and how it works to recognise the intelligence at work – and yet we, as mere humans, seem to think we know better.

I surrendered – not gave up – *surrendered* my will, my ego. I stopped fighting and allowed the wisdom both inside me and the wisdom of the Universe to take over. I stopped trying to hang on to my own ideas and ways of thinking. I gave in to a power greater than myself which resides inside myself and... the results have been far better than my rational mind could ever have conceived of.

Everything you want: peace, happiness, fulfilment, love, physical and emotional health is all right there inside you within your grasp. You don't have to acquire or learn anything... as a matter of fact, you must unlearn some things. You must clear away the old thinking patterns. Open your mind to what is possible in this Universe because the truth as I have experienced it, is that 'It' is more powerful than I as a mere mortal will ever be. The Universe in its infinite wisdom has a plan for you... and somewhere deep inside you know what you were created to do. Our upbringing, our conditioning, our culture, our world gets in the way of that but deep down, you know.

I know for myself when my head gets in the way I am in trouble! When I listen to that deeper, all-knowing part of myself I know that everything will work out in the most perfect way possible. And it does, but it's not usually the way my logical mind would have thought.

And please keep in mind here, I'm not special. Smart yes, but self-destructive, and I didn't have the benefit of money to help me figure any of this out, I felt too worthless to ask for help, I didn't go to counselling or therapy. I discovered this by myself. Trial and error, and having to accept the fact that my life was full of miracles I had no earthly explanation for. I had to believe... and I'm glad I did. It's led me on this path to inner peace, to being in flow with the Universe and this is what I want for you too. Please believe it IS possible for you too!

This is where the practice of meditation can help. Meditation by its very nature shuts down the conscious mind, the chatter. It quiets the gremlins and allows us to get to a deeper place. An all-knowing place within us where the true answers lie. It allows us to go to that Zero Point, the place where everything begins and where our truth is held. Where peace and contentment lie within us. It allows us to return our body and mind to the state of optimal performance. Your body knows how to function perfectly without the help of outside forces... if you can allow it to. Your mind knows exactly what chemicals, what signals to emit and when... if you allow it to.

The medical benefits of meditation have been proven: lower blood pressure, increased focus, increased calm, increased ability to handle day-to-day stressors. How? Because meditation allows us to go back to the state where our body and mind can function at their optimum level. And then the goal is learning to carry that with us throughout the day. That's why it's called a meditation practice. We'll discuss this more in the following chapters.

My dad always used to say to me: "Just go with the flow Susan, just go with the flow". I never understood what he meant until I started studying Spirituality and Quantum Physics.

The Universe is a flow, an infinitely intelligent place where energy constantly flows. When we can slip into that flow... when we can find our true selves and slip into that flow that is uniquely ours, then magic occurs. Nothing is difficult. Things fall into place. When we are not in the flow, when we are trying to live a life that is not in keeping with who we truly are, when we are trying to force our way in this world, we will always run into problems. I believe this is where our unhappiness comes from. And where a lot of our emotional and physical illness comes from.

We are trying to force ourselves into a life that is not ours and it causes us to become sick and unhappy.

Finding our true selves allows us to slip into that flow and things become easier.

Before we look at some spiritual truths, take a minute and think about:

- *Have you experienced miracles in your life?*
- *Have you experienced a time when you were "in flow"?*
- *What did it feel like? What were you doing?*
- *How might you recapture that? What do you need to let go of to tap into the Universal Wisdom available to all of us – inside of us?*

There's a story that I was told years ago – some of you are probably familiar with it so forgive me if my version is not completely accurate. It goes like this... there was a flood, and the flood waters were rising and there was this man standing on the roof of his house watching the flood waters rise. Someone came along with a boat and asked the man if he needed assistance as the flood waters were rising and he would die if he stayed where he was. "No thank you," he said. "God will save me". The flood waters kept rising and another boat came along and he was asked the same thing: "Can we help you? We have a boat and we can take you to safety". "No thank you," responded the man "God will look after me." Later, as the flood waters were getting dangerously high, a third boat came along offering to take the man to safety, and again the man gave the same answer. "No thank you, God will look after me". Well, the man drowned. And when he met God in heaven he asked God: "Why didn't you help me? I was waiting for you!" "What are you talking about?" said God. "I sent you three boats!"

I always remember this story as the partnership between the Universe and the Universe in human form. This world is full of miracles and opportunities... but it's our responsibility to recognise and seize them when they come along. YOU must raise your hand and say: "I'm ready".

Let's look at some spiritual principles that might help you "go with the flow" and find the peace, happiness and success that we all deserve in this Universe.

SECRET #EIGHT:

Universal Truths (Spirituality)

"The spiritual quest is not some added benefit to our life, something you embark on if you have the time and inclination. We are spiritual beings on an earthly journey. Our spirituality makes up our beingness."
John Bradshaw

"Spirituality is meant to take us beyond our tribal identity into a domain of awareness that is more universal."
Deepak Chopra

"Religion is for people who are scared to go to hell. Spirituality is for people who have already been there."
Bonnie Raitt

It's no surprise that I identify with the Bonnie Raitt quote. I have been to hell. There is a common saying in recovery: "They opened up the gates of hell to let me out". I do feel that way, I know what "hell" feels like, and if you're reading this book, I suspect you may do as well. It's time to come into the light. Now that we have looked at the science of all of this, we must turn our attention to the Spirituality aspect. The years of studying and learning and applying psychological principles, of creating my own Cognitive Behavioural Therapy techniques, absolutely worked. But they wouldn't have worked without the spiritual aspect. And trust me when I say, this was a hard one for me to grasp.

I *knew* there was something bigger out there operating but I didn't know what. As I've said before, I had just had too many miracles happen to me once I "woke-up". What happened to me in rehab can only be described as a spiritual awakening. I don't know what else to call it and for a long time I didn't understand it. Now I do.

There is a bigger plan for you...

There is a plan for you bigger than you know! How do I know? Because I see it in action every single day in my own life and in the lives of others with whom I work. The Universe doesn't make mistakes. You aren't a mistake. You were created for a reason... a purpose, it is our very human experience that gets in the way of that. Everything you want is waiting for you... you just need to get out of your own way long enough to go after it!

Remember the story of the chipmunk and the squirrel? It was about how our ego, our rational mind, can cause us to stand in our own way by believing we can't when in fact, we can.

It's high time we stopped letting our own self-limiting beliefs or our fear of failure, of not being perfect, dictate our future. We don't have to stay stuck in our unhappiness, self-hatred, misery and poverty. The only thing preventing us from achieving what we want is our belief about what is possible. This whole book has been about this very concept so adeptly demonstrated by the story of the chipmunk and the squirrel.

I knew that night in rehab there was a plan for me. I knew my life had been saved for a reason – why, I didn't know. Remember, at the time I was working in a ladies clothing store making minimum wage? What plan could there be for a low-life loser like me? But there was a plan.

How I Got Here, From There

After I sobered up I did exactly what I should have done – I followed the suggestions and that included sharing my story at meetings. I remember the first time I did this – I had never spoken in public before, I was terrified of people! And here I was, standing in front of 30 or so people having to tell them what happened to me. I felt like I was going to die... but I was doing it anyway because I had learned that everything I thought I knew was wrong. So I was practising the habit of not listening to the voice in my head, but listening to the voice of others instead. When I was asked to speak and share my experiences with a group – I did. I had no idea what I would say or why they would want to listen to me... but I did it. And I was so afraid I felt like I was going to die.

I have no idea what I said that night. All I know is that afterward people came up to me and thanked me, they said they couldn't believe an hour had passed, they were completely engrossed in the story. This was confounding to me! Who would want to listen to me? And yet they had. This was my first clue about the divine plan waiting for me – which, of course, I ignored for a few more years.

Fast forward a couple of years, and I was ready to leave my job in the ladies clothing store (I was manager by this point) and move to an office job. My self-esteem was rising, my confidence was rising, and I was trained to be a really good secretary, so I was sure I could do it if someone would give me the chance. I've told you the story of applying to the Temporary Agency so I could get some recent office experience and they hired me in the office. One of the questions they asked me was: "Have you ever done any Customer Service training?" Well! I had been in retail for a few years and has risen to manager which meant not only had I done a lot of Customer Service training but I had to train the people I hired so... I took a leap... I said "Yes", and before I knew it, I was doing Customer Service training for the new-hires for that account that I was working on.

The very first session I did I was again terrified. My self-talk was about to tank me: "Who do you think you're kidding? You've never done this before! You don't know what you're talking about! No one will want to listen to you... " and on it went. BUT, I had nothing to lose. In my mind, I shouldn't have got the job anyway, so if they found out that I was a big loser and didn't know what I was talking about, then there was no harm because in my ego driven mind I was sure that's what was going to happen eventually anyway.

I probably don't have to tell you what happened in that first Customer Service training session but I will: the participants loved it! I did the training, told stories, I included some of the information that I was learning in college (I was constantly in school learning about how to be a functioning human being) and I was funny and they loved it! I was a hit! Again… I didn't understand how that could be, but I was not listening to the voice in my head, I was looking at the evidence.

This is a powerful technique because our mind plays some pretty sophisticated tricks on us. I had got into the habit of not listening to myself but instead looking at the evidence, at the facts… not what I thought but what the facts were telling me. And in this case, the facts in the form of evaluation sheets and participant feedback were telling me I was good! It was hard for me to believe even though the evidence was right there in front of me and so I pushed it away, I dismissed it as "it's only one session". And then it happened again and again and I eventually had to accept the fact that whether I liked it or not, whether I believed it or not, I was good at this Customer Service training.

It was about a year and a half later that my father died. By this time, I was a Major Account Manager with the very huge responsibility of the performance, hiring, firing and welfare of 225 people. As I have said, my father's passing rocked me to the core to the point where I thought about committing suicide. All the years spent studying psychology had taught me that his passing was a major life event for me, and if I didn't grieve properly, it would have the capacity to have a lasting effect on my life. Well, by then I was an expert at how unresolved issues and unspoken emotions can drive someone to make some self-destructive choices so I took a week off work to grieve and go to a grief counsellor. (It's funny to me now that in my human arrogance I really believed I could *plan* how to grieve). Needless to say, a week wasn't enough and I ended up taking short-term leave.

The sense of freedom from my conditioning that I had felt upon my father's passing has stayed with me. It's always present. This freedom to choose… freedom to do anything I wanted. The problem was, at that time, I didn't know what I wanted. It was time for me to do something different, the challenge in my current position was gone and it was time for me to move on. I could feel the push. But move on to what?

School, books, and workshops had proven to be an inspiration for me so I bought a book, *What Colour is Your Parachute*, to try to learn how to figure out what I should do next. In the back of my mind, always present, was the knowledge that I had to give back... I had to pay the Universe back for my second chance so it had to be something involving people and helping. I knew that. I also knew I was restless, I needed challenge, I needed to be able to travel like the executives in my company and, there had to be equal parts physical and mental stimulation.

I made a list of these job requirements. And then I made another list. I made a list of all the things I was good at. My natural talents if you will. This was hard because I had to go outside of myself to do this. I didn't believe I was good at anything except screwing up my life. Oh... and sewing. I was good at sewing. But that was it in my opinion, so I stepped out of myself and made a list of what other people said I was good at. What it came down to was: people. Funny if you think about it. The thing I was most terrified of was the very thing I was best at. I could connect with people. I could gain people's trust very quickly and develop relationships very quickly. It made me really good at sales. I could speak in front of a large group and connect with them and hold their attention. I was good at training and coaching and counselling. It made me a good leader, a good manager. Hmmm... social worker? Nope. Don't have the patience. So what else could I do that was in line with my natural abilities and would meet the requirements I needed in a job? I was stuck.

For weeks, I read the job ads in the newspapers, I went to classes and searched in the library for job titles that I thought might appeal to me. Nothing. And then it hit me: Human Resources! I should work in Human Resources!

At this point, if you are thinking that the job I was describing 20 or so years ago is the exact career I have today, you are correct. The point here is that 20 or so years ago I didn't know that "professional speaker" was a job. I had never seen one. Never met one. Never seen one advertised. I was limited by my own experience, my own view of the world and what is and was possible.

So Human Resources it was. And again, I started researching and found out that you could specialise in Human Resources and one of the specialties was training! I had found my niche – or so I thought. I decided this is what I would do, even telling my bosses that this was my intention: to get a job in training and, since after all I was (OK fine, still am) a perfectionist, I was going to be the best trainer I could be and go for yet more schooling, to a university for a Diploma in Adult Education. Imagine my surprise when the company Vice President offered to pay for the schooling! I won't go into the turmoil that this caused in me... being a people-pleaser meant I didn't want to turn her down, but taking her offer in my mind came with a price – I would have to stay working with that company which is not something I wanted to do. And somewhere deep inside me was a very small voice that said: "You should start your own business". Of course, I kept it at the back of my mind because that was a ridiculous idea, "people like us don't do that". But it was there nonetheless.

I ended up splitting the cost of university with my company, I stayed there for another nine months and then I left to work in training. After a few months, the small voice deep inside me that said "start your own business" became not so small. It took over my thinking, my focus, and became too loud to ignore, and so one day I committed. I would start my own business and I quit my job. There were a few very scary months of not knowing if I would be able to pay my rent or feed myself, but the urge to do this was so strong I couldn't ignore it – I knew not to ignore it – I had to put it to rest. So I tried my best. I had very little knowledge and experience in how to get a business going, and just as I was about to give in to the "see... who do you think you are... this isn't going to work... people like us don't do this" I got a phone call from someone I had worked with. She had changed jobs and she was looking for someone to do Customer Service training for her client and she remembered that I was "a very good trainer". Was I interested? *The Universe always has a plan... we just have to be open to it.*

That one contract kept me financially stable for one year. Long enough to get more clients, get experience and cement my business.

And if you're thinking *"you were lucky"*, I don't believe in luck. It was, as it always has been, the Universe providing. I needed to put myself out there, to show that I was willing and ready to do what it took, and I have never looked back.

My practice of following that small inside voice, my practice of not listening to my own self-talk but looking at the evidence, my practice of not buying into my fear, my practice of trusting that the Universe has a grander plan for me than I will ever know has paid off.

I have continued to grow, to develop, to change. I trust that whoever or whatever it was that gave me a second chance did not do it for nothing. There was a reason, and as long as I trust, I will never go without. I have proven that to myself time and time again. **And whoever you are, for whatever reason you picked up this book... the same is true for you. There is a plan and this is all part of that plan.**

That small voice you hear is your true self, your higher self. It is the voice that knows who you really are and what you really want. The problem is the voice is quiet. The ego is loud, it yells, it dominates, it reasons. The higher self is quiet. It whispers: "Look at that... go here... read that book... leave your job..." And which voice do we listen to? The loud one of course! But it's not helping you. It's keeping you safe, keeping you stuck, not wanting you to fail. All success comes with failure. You have to make mistakes to learn and grow. Listen to the quiet voice. What does the quiet voice tell you?

I have to stop and ask at this point – do you ever hear that very small voice from deep inside you?

- *What is it telling you to do?*
- *What do you do with the voice? Listen to it? Dismiss or ignore it? Tell yourself it's crazy, you can't do whatever it's telling you to do because...*

We all have that voice, that knowingness. After all, we are the Universe and the Universe is us.

It's a Partnership...

There is a saying in Spirituality: if you have a need it's because the Universe is preparing to fill it. But we must put ourselves out there to get it. The Universe is us and we are the Universe. It's a partnership. The Universe is not going to bust through your door and drag you off the couch to do something, but it's there, quietly waiting for you. You must go out and meet it. It's a partnership. You must be willing to take the risk... take the step... and let the Universe take care of the rest.

Here's how I always think about it: I think about it like a baseball game. As a baseball player, it's my job to suit up, show up, and hit the ball as hard as I can. Where the ball lands is not up to me. This is my metaphor for life.

Suit up, show up and do your best. Let go of the outcome. Sometimes it will work out, sometimes it works out in a very different way than how you thought it would, and sometimes it doesn't work out because we're not on the right path... yet. You didn't get the job you applied for? It wasn't the right job, or the right time. You tried to start a business and it failed? You weren't ready yet, or maybe it's the wrong business for you or in the wrong place on the planet. We have to do our best every day. We have to say "yes" to opportunities, we have to go out and meet the world half-way. Whatever happens... you just need to look at yourself in the mirror at night and ask: "Did I do the best job possible today?" And if the answer is yes then you've done your part. When it doesn't work out it's not a failure... it's a sign – "look over here", "not yet", "learn more". It's not failure. It's an opportunity to learn, to grow, and to do it differently next time.

You ALWAYS Have a Choice...

Whatever we put out there is what we will get back. I've said this a few times throughout this book. So let's talk about what this really means. The life we are currently leading is a by-product of our choices. We create our existence and experience. Now I know some of you are arguing with me right now but hear me out – it is *never* what happens to us. It's always our choice as to how to react! One of the most frustrating things that I hear (and believe me, I too have been guilty of saying this in the past) is, "It's not my fault, that's the way I am." Or, "I can't help it, it's just the way I am." Well... if you can't help it then who can? Giving up your power to circumstance is being a victim. Giving up your power to the conditioning, situations and circumstances in your life is just wrong. It creates misery and unhappiness and keeps us stuck in that invisible prison!

When you do this, what you are saying is that you are a victim. No one likes a victim, although I believe some are very comfortable playing that role.

Accepting this responsibility is hard. I know. Prior to sobering up I blamed *everything* that happened to me, *everything* that was wrong with me, on my mother. It was her fault. All of it was her fault. I had nothing to do with it. It all happened to me because of her. The truth is it wasn't her fault. She is just who she is. She didn't consciously *do* anything to me, she was just doing what parents do – the best she could, given her experience and circumstance. So I was faced with a choice: I could either choose to continue the way I was, playing the victim in my life, OR, I could choose to change it.

I could learn to think differently, respond differently, communicate differently. And I did. I took responsibility for my own actions. I did all those things to myself. No one forced me to become property of a gang. No one forced me to move away from home. I had plenty of opportunities to receive medical help – I was the one who refused to talk, who refused to tell the truth. It was all me. My choice. That was hard to accept. But once I did accept it, I could begin to look at the choices I had made and make different ones.

Whether you like it or not you have created your current situation – whatever that is. You have made choices that have led you to this place. What kind of choices? I don't know... that would be personal. Only you know.

I know for myself, my ending up on the street was a choice. It didn't just magically happen. I was in pain. The emotional pain that came from wanting to please my parents and make them proud but at the same time knowing that doing what they expected me to do was not who I was. I was in emotional pain from believing that I had to be perfect all the time, that I had to be all things to all people all the time. When the pain became too unbearable… I checked out. I chose to drown it with alcohol which led to drugs. I chose to numb myself to protect myself from the pain. That was my choice. I was responsible for that.

I chose to stay with an abusive partner. If you have read my book *An Invisible Prison* you will know that one of the most influential people in my life was my abusive partner. And his influence didn't go away for many years even after I left him. He abused me horribly. Emotionally and physically. I threatened to leave on many occasions and I even did leave once or twice. But I always went back. I chose to stay with my partner. Why? Because I was afraid… afraid he was right, that I was a low-life, good-for-nothing, worthless piece of garbage. I was afraid that no one else would ever want me. I was afraid that I wasn't good enough, that I was unlovable. I was afraid… so I told myself I had to stay with him. I told myself I didn't have a choice. Of course I had a choice! I just didn't like my choices and so chose to believe I didn't have any.

This is so common today… I see it all the time in the corporations I work with – people who hate their jobs. They are so unhappy and miserable it's not only affecting their emotional health but their physical health as well. When I speak with them about their situation they readily admit how unhappy they are, how unhealthy the situation is, how it is affecting their personal lives and their families. But when I bring up the idea of leaving the job the answer is always the same: "I can't. I have a family to support!" Or, with some people it's: "I can't! I have a pension." Well, here's the thing folks – yes, you CAN leave. You are choosing not to. You are letting money guide your choices. And if you choose to do that, then that is OK. But please, recognise it for what it is – a choice. Which is my nice way of saying: "Quit complaining about it!"

You can leave your job, your partner, your house, your town. You can leave your parents, your siblings, or change your friends. You do not have to do anything in this life you don't want to except die. You don't even have to pay taxes. You would be choosing between paying taxes and going to jail but the choice remains. We have choices.

When we tell ourselves "I don't have a choice", it's really code for "I have choices, but I don't like my choices so I'll stay doing what I'm doing."

I'll give you a minute to think about that.

What you need to know is that from a spiritual standpoint we will continue to repeat a lesson until we learn it. We will create the same circumstances until we learn to make different choices. And, if you believe in reincarnation as I do, you need to know that just because your body dies it doesn't mean the lesson dies with it. You carry these lessons through lifetime after lifetime until you learn the lesson, until you make a different choice.

So it is possible that some of the unfortunate situations you are faced with in this lifetime are karmic in nature. They are leftovers from a past life and they will persist until you make a different choice in this lifetime.

Take a few minutes to contemplate:

- *What circumstances or situations are you unhappy with?*
- *What choices have you made that have led you to this place?*
- *What choices do you need to make to free yourself?*

Note that there may be more than one choice, there are likely many, but we must proceed one at a time. This work is not a destination, it's a journey, a pilgrimage if you will, a pilgrimage home to our true selves – happy, peaceful and abundant. We're inside just waiting to emerge... waiting for all the surface stuff to be cleared away so our true light can shine through.

You always have a choice even if sometimes you don't like the options.

The Universe Rewards Action...

The Universe rewards action. Our challenge is that we get so confused between the loud ego voice telling us: "Don't do that! You're crazy! That will never work...", and the quiet, all-knowing, higher-self voice which whispers: "Write a book", "Apply for that job", "Start your own business", "Move to Liverpool". In our confusion, of course, we listen to the rational, logical voice and we believe the quiet, whispering voice, the longing voice, to be just a wish, or a secret desire. Yes, it's a wish and a secret desire but it's also direction! It's the voice of peace and happiness! The voice that *knows* what you are supposed to do on this planet!

We weren't put here to be miserable, to fail. We weren't created or reincarnated to live a life of misery, poverty and negativity. If those things are happening, it's because we created our reality from our choices. We have free will which is both a good and a bad thing. There are no dark forces – there is only the absence of light. And a lot of us (myself included) have spent a lot of time and energy trying to dim or hide our light. It's time to uncover it! It's time to clear away the thoughts and beliefs that are keeping you imprisoned! It's time to let your light shine! Listen to the voice! Follow the steps. The Universe rewards action – any action no matter how small will bring you a positive reward. It will bring you closer to where you are destined to be.

Here's how it works: when we want to make a change, the very human part of ourselves insists on seeing the plan. We want to see the whole path, the whole staircase if you will… we want to see what it looks like when the change is made. We want guarantees of success or we are not going to make the change. But that's not how it works! It's so profoundly painful for people to make life changes because of this. We will explore this further in the next chapter

We must take the first step. That's all. That small voice is pointing you in the right direction. Your job is to take that first step, whatever it is: do research, speak to someone about starting a business, complete the application, send in your CV, start believing that this is possible – whatever it is, no matter how small, we just have to take the first step. Then, and only then, the next step will be revealed.

You can see how this would prevent a lot of us from making the changes and doing the things we say we want? We can't see how it's going to work out so our ego goes into protection mode. "Don't do that! It's not going to work!" it says. But your ego doesn't know. As I have talked about, we often behave or make choices based on our perceptions, which we believe to be the truth. When your ego tells you: "It's not going to work!" it doesn't really know that to be true. It's just trying to keep you safe. Trust. Trust the infinite wisdom of the Universe. Trust that once you take that first step, the next step will reveal itself. And then the next, and the next. You are looked after. You have a path. You just have to trust and take the first step. You will be rewarded.

What is your quiet voice telling you?

What is one action you can take today to move closer to your dream?

What is one small step you can take?

When the Student is Ready, the Teacher Appears...

There will always be a reason for people to come into your life – either you need them to change your life or they need you to change theirs. Everyone has something to teach us. Every relationship you have is a mirror for you, telling you something about yourself. You don't have to like what you see, but hopefully you can see it as a sign that change is necessary. You can use your relationships to see what choices you are making, and begin to make better ones.

Are you being used or taken advantage of? Are you not treated with respect? Does someone take you for granted? You have created this and it's yours to fix. Everyone in your life now, and in the future, will teach you something if you pay attention. I have constant teachers in mine... my mother is a powerful source of learning for me. And for that I'm grateful.

Occasionally, you will meet people seemingly randomly who will have a profound effect on your life.

My life was going just fine. I had created a wonderful career for myself, I had written my book *An Invisible Prison* which took five years but I did it, and it took another two years to have it published. I had everything any person could want... and I was miserable. The Universe had come knocking again. I was slipping into a depression, I could feel it, and I knew

I needed to pull myself out of it. I even knew how – I needed challenge. I needed to take the next step but I had no idea what that was. *This isn't entirely true – I did know what the next step was, but once again it felt so overwhelming and impossible that I pushed it away.*

And this is where I had a profound experience with "when the student is ready, the teacher will appear". I'll say it again: every person who comes into your life comes in for a reason – either they are there to teach you something, or you are there to teach them. Sometimes they come in for a brief time, and sometimes they come in for a long time. Sometimes the encounter is pleasant and sometimes not so pleasant, but everyone who comes into your life serves a purpose for you. I always say, if it wasn't for my abusive ex coming into my life I would not have the life I have today. He pushed me to my limit, he pushed me to have to choose: die or fight. I fought. My parents, each in their own way, taught me things. They gave me the lessons I would have to learn in this life. I was born to my parents for a reason… so I could learn these lessons. And it was my first spiritual teacher who helped me understand this.

My work was providing amazing opportunities, and I was saying yes to anything new and different to stretch myself, to try to fight off this depression, including travelling. I was with a client for two weeks but had the weekend to myself. There was a conference a couple of states away about publishing and speaking as a career – I decided to go.

I went to the conference, sat in on some of the lectures, browsed the booths to see what people were offering, but still I wasn't sure any of it was for me. At that time, while I had confidence in what I did for a living, I still did not have a lot of confidence in myself. I mean… who else would publish a book and then not tell anyone? That should give you some idea of the level of confidence I had in my personal life. Professionally, as a trainer I was fine. But Sue the person… not so fine. There was something I was supposed to do, I knew it had to do with writing and speaking, but I was so busy ducking it, bobbing and weaving to avoid looking at the next step because it was so outlandish in my mind, that I missed what was right in front of my face. Enter my first spiritual teacher.

One speaker, a woman, whom I went to hear, I didn't like very much. As a matter of fact, I did my usual, took a back-row seat near the exit just in case I wanted to leave and started to listen to the presentation. She was talking about the Universe, and how we all had a calling... "a cosmic package" to deliver. Well I listened for about 10 minutes to this "divine purpose", "divine discomfort" talk, and left. I mean... what did any of that have to do with publishing or marketing a book? I went outside to her booth and proceeded to grill the poor girl standing behind the table: Who is this woman? What does she do? Why is she here? I was trying to figure out exactly what this woman could offer. I didn't get an answer I liked. She offered "packages". But I didn't want a package. I wanted someone to tell me what to do next! Sound familiar?

Oh, the depths of my denial. The depths of my "my way or nothing". Once again I was trying, in my desperation, to get some relief from my suffering, to force my way onto the Universe. I was trying my best to find the quickest, shortest way to the next step, to stop my misery. I just wanted to be happy and challenged again. I just wanted someone to tell me what to do. But I already knew what to do. I didn't really need anyone to tell me, I needed someone to coax it out of me, to help me believe it, to be my mirror so I could separate what my logical mind told me from the truth that was in my heart.

I left that conference with nothing but a few brochures. One of them was from the lady PhD I had heard speaking because, let's face it, the seed had been planted. I was supposed to go to that conference because my next teacher was there waiting for me. But I'm a bit rebellious, so sometimes with me it takes a while...

Nothing in my life changed, it just got worse. I felt worse. I was desperate and the voice in my head kept saying: "Call that lady... call that lady", that lady being the one from the publishing conference. And so finally, when I was in enough pain, I called to see if I could get a coaching session. "She doesn't do private coaching, she has 'packages' or workshops..." Ugh. I just wanted to talk to her so I pushed it. Well, I eventually heard back. She agreed to speak with me.

A few weeks later the appointed call time arrived. Right in the middle of a workshop for me in a different state, and as it turned out, in the middle of a wicked storm. I couldn't get through to the number I was given, I was running around the building trying to find a signal on my mobile, and when I finally got through I was in a real state!

The first thing she said to me was: "Wow... there's a lot of drama with you isn't there?" I wasn't sure I was going to enjoy this, and while I may not have enjoyed it, she changed my life in that call. She told me I was never supposed to die, I chose to "come back to the planet and do this. I chose this life. I came out of retirement to come back and take this on." And while none of this made any logical sense to me, it did make sense to me. I knew her words to be true. While my logical brain was not understanding, the other part of me – the part that had woken up in rehab – understood perfectly. She told me that to move to the next phase I needed to drop "the story". I had no idea what she meant by that, and it took almost seven years for me to finally get it.

That phone call began my relationship with my very first spiritual teacher. She told me I had got myself from A to B, and I needed her to help me get from B to C. She was right. The lessons I learned through my years of studying with her were transformational lessons about my own self-esteem and confidence. She was a very powerful, although sometimes not pleasant, mirror for me. A very powerful teacher who provided me with some life-changing lessons.

Give it some thought: what teachers have appeared in your life? I have had many... my mother, who is a big mirror for me, my father in the lessons I learned after his passing, my abusive ex who taught me so many things that pushed me to the limits and caused me to fight for myself, my spiritual teachers who opened doors to other ways of thinking and being, my best friend who gives me a model of behaviour to aspire to...

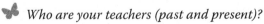 *Who are your teachers (past and present)?*

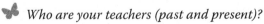 *What have you learned/are you learning from them?*

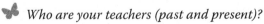 *How do they serve you?*

The Law of Alignment

This brings us right back to the beginning of this chapter – there is a bigger plan for you. However, for this plan to unfold, we must be aware of the Law of Alignment. We must live in keeping with who we truly are.

Underneath all the conditioning, belief systems, values and morals imprinted upon you by people outside of yourself lies a divine spirit, a divine human being, perfect just the way you are. We all have our own unique talents and abilities, our own inherent knowledge that has been covered up over the years by this world's ideas of what you should and should not be. You don't need to gain anything; you don't need to change who you are... you need to uncover who you are.

Most of us have heard of the Law of Attraction, but what's often not mentioned is the Law of Alignment. The Law of Attraction works, without a doubt. The problem is you must be in alignment for it to work. Here's what I mean: I can create a vision board for winning a million dollars, I can have pictures of boats and houses and fabulous vacations on the board. I can visualise and meditate on it and send my request out into the Universe. BUT... if I don't believe I deserve a million dollars, if somewhere inside of me I don't believe this will happen... then no amount of visioning, meditating, praying or wishing will bring it about.

Everything you want is out there waiting for you! Waiting for you to catch up, waiting for you to live in alignment with who you truly are, waiting for you to make choices that are in keeping with your divine self, and the closer you move to alignment, the more you will be able to attract or manifest.

That is the whole point of this book. Learning to clear away any thoughts, beliefs or behaviours that don't serve you, that aren't in line with who you truly are. Once we can do this, magic starts to happen. The Law of Attraction begins to spontaneously occur once we begin to move into alignment with our divine nature.

I'd ask you who you really are, but you already know. You are your talents and abilities no matter how silly you think they are. Give it some thought...

What are your natural talents and abilities? What are those things you just do well, you don't have to think about, you just do? We all have them, but sometimes we don't see them as gifts because they are so natural to us, we just do them, and so our human mind assumes that because it's so easy for us, it's easy for everyone. This is not true.

In my exercise to list my natural talents and abilities I had to put down that I can speak to an audience, I can connect with them on an emotional level very quickly. This did not seem like a talent to me. I did not realise this was a gift. I thought everyone could do this. It wasn't until I worked in sales and someone accused me of having "horseshoes up my..." – you know where – that I had to stop and look at this. I watched what other people were doing and then I watched what I was doing. I could connect, build trust very rapidly with people, communicate with them in a way that made sense to them, even strangers, which meant I always had the highest sales.

As I watched other sales people, I saw that some could not connect with people. I didn't understand why I could do this and others couldn't but there it was... a natural talent for me. And I have come to understand that at my very core, it is who I am. This is what I do. This is my gift. Divine Self Expression through speaking and writing and the Divine Power to show people what they are capable of, to help others find their way on this journey. These are my energy centres. This book, my workshops and my seminars are me, in alignment with my authentic self, sharing not what I've studied but what I have lived, learned and *know* to be true.

Each of us has these natural talents and abilities. Are you a builder, a baker, do you enjoy working with your hands? Are you a nurturer? Are you the "wise one" always offering the truth? Are you compassionate? Can you see the reality in situations that others can't? We all have unique and inherent abilities that sometimes we don't recognise and/or value because we've always been this way. The challenge is to recognise them and capitalise on them. Try to find a way to utilise these gifts positively. This is being in alignment and this is where the Law of Attraction can work its magic!

We must stop letting the outside world dictate our inner circumstances. I was raised to be a really good secretary, but thank goodness for my rebellious streak! My choice of careers may not be conventional, it may not be easily understandable, and yes, most of my family still has no idea what I do for a living, but I have been doing it successfully for over 20 years. Simply because I am in alignment with my authentic self. You can achieve this too, but you must know who you are at soul level first.

What are you good at? What can you do well that other people struggle with? Start to notice throughout the day:

- *What tasks or activities make you happy?*
  When are you "in the zone"?
- *When work is easy for you, what are you doing?*
  What do you like to do?

Start to notice as you go through the day what makes you happy, what makes you unhappy. What are the things you do well that you don't have to think about? If you get stuck, ask your family or the people closest to you. Sometimes we can't see our talents, we take them for granted, so ask others. They will be aware of who you are and what you are good at. This is a good start for getting back to who you truly are.

You will find some further information at the back of the book under 'Additional Resources'.

SECRET #NINE:

How to Manifest The Life You Desire

"The Law of Attraction states that all forms of matter and energy are attracted to that which is of a like vibration. The implications of this law are vast, and the law holds true for all known Universes. "That which is like unto itself is drawn." The thoughts we hold attract similar thoughts and become large masses of thought called thoughtforms. The general vibration that a person holds is representative of the balance of their thoughts. As we become aware or conscious of our thoughts, we can raise our vibration by setting forth thoughts that are more in harmony with our desires. When our thoughts are in harmony with our highest desires, we are filled with joy and ecstasy. When we learn to set forth our thoughts consciously, we are no longer victims of our own outdated programming. We increasingly attract thought of a higher vibration and raise the level of thought at which we habitually vibrate."

Abraham (Esther & Jerry Hicks)

Even as I write this I can feel the resistance of some of you who are reading this. Wanting to believe, but somehow believing it's only possible for me... not for you. Nothing could be further from the truth – I am you! I have been there... I have travelled this path and I have participated in taking my life from one of poverty and misery to one that I never imagined was possible. And I'm here to help you do the same thing. Is it easy? Yes and no. It's easy because all it requires is a change in thinking, making some

different choices, and taking action – any action. It's hard because all it requires is a change in thinking, making some different choices, and taking action – any action.

If you were to come to me with a problem or complaint about your life or your job I would only ask one question: What have you tried to do about it? Because as I've said all along we are the creators of our existence. We authored our life story... yes, things have happened to us along the way, some of them not pleasant. But here's the thing: what do we do with those experiences? Do we use them to continue to justify our attitudes, behaviours and actions? Or do we say: "OK, this happened, now let me move past it..."? If you are in emotional pain, unhappy, dissatisfied with your life, you CAN change it! You have the power...

> *"When the pain of your current existence outweighs the fear of change and the unknown, you will take action."*
> **Susan Armstrong**

> *"With an open mind I can accept that anything is possible."*
> **Rozine**

When faced with any problem there are only three possible solutions: accept it, change it, or get rid of it. Unfortunately, when it comes to life circumstances, sometimes we are very unhappy and can't accept them, but we don't believe we can change them and we tell ourselves we can't get rid of them. That's how we keep ourselves stuck! But we can change them... we can even choose to accept them and to see things a different way.

As the Abraham quote at the beginning of this section states:

> *"The thoughts we hold attract similar thoughts and become large masses of thought called thoughtforms. The general vibration that a person holds is representative of the balance of their thoughts. As we become aware or conscious of our thoughts, we can raise our vibration by setting forth thoughts that are more in harmony with our desires."*

This is something we look at in Soul Realignment work (which is the process of understanding who you are at a Soul level). Any thought when repeated over and over will grow. You will feed it. You give it energy through constant focus on it and eventually accept it as truth. We can create thoughtforms that occupy our emotional or mental bodies and direct our actions and behaviours. The thoughtforms are subconscious and may be such a part of our existence that we are not even aware they are there... but they are, and they are causing us to stand in our way. They are part of the emotional prison we create for ourselves.

A woman once came to see me who was miserable. She had a good job, she owned her own home, and she was miserable. She wanted me to help her. As we talked she revealed she had no friends, "no life" as she put it. She was in her early 50s and had never had a relationship. All she did was go to work and then look after her parents. Her parents were ageing, still living in their own home and needing assistance. I asked her why she didn't go out and make friends, why she didn't take a day and look after herself? For every question I asked she had an excuse... her parents needed her, she was an only child, there was no one else to look after them, she couldn't commit to going out with friends because she would be worried about her parents, she couldn't have a relationship because it would take focus away from her parents.

It didn't matter what I said, she had a reason why my ideas wouldn't work. She was choosing to give her life up for her parents. Everything revolved around them. This was her choice. She could have got a carer, but: "No one would know how to look after them as well as I can..." After two sessions, I gave up. No one can help someone who doesn't want to be helped. That's the first rule: for you, your life, your circumstances to change, you must *WANT* to change them. It is *your* life. No one else's. You can't live it for someone else. You can't live your life wishing it were different... well you can I suppose... but it doesn't work. You have to want to change it *and* act to change it.

A couple of years after I tried to help this woman, she sent me an email. Her parents had died and she wanted to know what she should do now? It was heart breaking... she was 55 years old, with no friends, no relationship, no family. I cried when I read her email, but (and I hate that this is going to sound the way it's going to sound) she created this through choice and only she could choose to change things for herself, but she didn't. Now she was forced to live with her choice.

I received another email from someone who told me very genuinely in her unhappiness that she thought life was about "making your way through life without hurting people". Well, that's a sure-fire way to create misery! And I know exactly what that's like! As a recovering people-pleasing perfectionist, I can attest to the fact that living your life to make other people happy will bring nothing but unhappiness to you!

You must become aware of the thoughts you are giving energy to. You have created your own thoughtforms and they may very well be guiding your life. The question is, are they helping you or hindering you? This is how we manifest – we believe that good things will happen. We set our intention, our knowing, of what we want to occur and we let go, we let the Universe do the rest. Someone asked what the difference was between a wish and an intention. The answer is simple: a wish means "I hope it happens", an intention is "it will happen". So set your intention and then let it go. The Universe knows what to do!

Take Back Your Life and Set Yourself Free

One of the most important things in manifesting the life you desire is to take back your life! Stop giving your power away to people, places, things, situations... every time you twist yourself into a pretzel to make someone else happy, you have given up your power to that person. Every time you replay a conversation or an argument in your head, you have given up your power to that person. Every time you are wishing and having expectations about a place you are going to or something you are doing, you are giving up your power to that place or experience. Every time you give up what you want for the sake of others – whether that be family, children, friends, co-workers, you are giving up your power.

In order to manifest the life you want, the first thing is to figure out *what do you want*? How much of your life, circumstances, situation is what *you want* and how much of it was scripted for you by others?

Take some time and give that some thought. It's not an easy exercise. For some, you have never thought about what YOU want before. Some of you have, and you don't know what you want. That's OK, doing the work in this book will help you figure it out. Later we'll talk about a couple of techniques that might help, but for now, think about it: if you could wave a magic wand what would your life look like?

- *Who are you? What do you look like? How do you spend your time?*
- *What is your ideal career (where you would be really happy and it wouldn't feel like a job)?*
- *Where do you live?*
- *What does your home look like?*
- *Who is around you?*
- *Are you married? Single? Dating? Who are you in a relationship with?*

At this point I think it's only fair to come clean and say that I too, am stuck in this right now. It's time for a change for me, so as I write this book, I too am practising these very concepts I'm telling you about. I'm starting with one step at a time. One foot in front of the other. One small step every day (and if I'm good at managing my time - several small steps every day) toward the next phase of my life. What will it look like? I don't know. I have a vision that I have sent out to the Universe. I have set my intention and am focusing on it and paying attention through taking an action toward it every day. But what will the result be? I don't know. For me, I always think about my life as a movie, and I can't wait to see what's next.

Overcoming the Fear of Change

For things to change, for your circumstances to get better, you must *WANT* to change. You must want take the first step. You have the power to create change in your life. One thought, one action done differently, will send different energy out into the Universe and you will get something different back. But just complaining, or wishing things were different, doesn't work. Action does.

This is where people get stuck, so let's talk a little bit about change… and more specifically, the fear involved in change.

We touched on this briefly in a previous chapter, but fear is such a powerful emotion that it warrants more time spent on it. Fear, if we let it, can keep us stuck. It can paralyse us. There is a saying that the greatest of human fears is the fear of public speaking, but this is not true! The greatest of human fears is the fear of the unknown, and change brings with it the unknown – uncertainty. We don't know what will happen, we can't predict the future and that makes us afraid. Our minds start to wander and worry. The "what ifs" start to take over, and before we know it, we've talked ourselves out of the change we intended to make.

Recall that acronym about fear: **F**alse **E**vidence **A**ppearing **R**eal. Back to the Centre of the Universe condition – most of the things you are afraid of reside only in your mind. We conjure up potential outcomes, situations and circumstances and then project them on to reality. And then… we behave as if they are facts! This is crazy! We can't possibly know the future! And yet… we prophesise the most horrific outcomes and then behave as if they have already happened! This is how we stay stuck in our invisible prison.

I remember when it came time for me to leave rehab, I was terrified! I was such a different person and everything I did was new to me. I had conjured up all these images of what could go wrong and worked myself up into a real state about it. This is what we do… we engage in these fantasies to the point that we end up paralysed. Too afraid of what might happen to take a chance and do something new!

In my case, I really didn't have a choice… I couldn't stay in rehab forever. I had to go back to my life. What I was going back to I didn't know. And this is the hard part. Any change you make will create discomfort, but what you need to remember is that this isn't bad! You can't have change without discomfort, it takes work. Think about it… how many of you can't sleep in a hotel bed? Why? Because it's not *your* bed… you're out of your comfort zone and it's **UN**comfortable. We think being uncomfortable or not knowing means something is wrong. It doesn't. It just means something is different.

When we desire to make a change it's like jumping off a cliff. Here you are, in your comfortable routine. Whether you are happy or unhappy doesn't matter. You are comfortable. You know exactly what is going to happen. You can predict the future – if I do this, then this, if I do that, then that. It's comfortable. You are familiar with it. You know how it works. And now you want to change. You are going jump off the cliff of your comfortable existence and try to make it to the next cliff. Where? ... Oh no... you don't know what's there! You don't know what will happen! You can't see the future or predict the outcome! This is scary! It's enough to make people stay where they are... even if they are miserable. It's that old saying: "The devil that you know is better than the devil that you don't know". But is it???

I'm not trying to scare you off change. Quite the opposite... I'm trying to let you know that the not knowing, the discomfort, the making mistakes as you find your way to the other side is NORMAL! And it is to be expected. If you aren't uncomfortable, if you aren't making mistakes, you are not changing and growing. You are stuck.

The discomfort will not last forever, but it's not pleasant being in that state so you need to find something to remind you of the goal. The temptation to go back to the nice, safe life/person you know is strong – but it's not the path to happiness, peace and/or success. To reach that, you must experience and be comfortable with some discomfort.

As uncomfortable as change is, it is necessary to move forward. The Universe will not let you fail! The uncertainty is a test of faith. Faith in the Universe, faith in yourself, faith in the plan... you must have faith. This is why the exercises in this book are so important. As you begin to raise your self-esteem and confidence levels you will begin to trust yourself and your abilities. The stronger it gets the more you know you can handle whatever happens. This is where control becomes an issue – control freaks (and I can say this because this is one of my recurring issues!) are afraid that they can't handle the unknown... they won't be able to deal with the things they can't predict. When you trust yourself you no longer worry about the unknown because you trust you can handle whatever comes your way. This is why self-esteem is your secret weapon. The more you have, the easier it is to handle change.

Here's an unfortunate truth: the Universe does not like a vacuum. As soon as you let go of the old something new will appear. But this means we must first let go of what no longer serves us... that's the unfortunate part. The good news is that something better is on the way! You just have to let go for long enough to allow what's next to appear and that can be very hard. I have told you the story of starting my own company. Just when I thought I couldn't go on anymore... just when I thought I would have to go back to a regular job, I got that phone call about call centre training and it was enough to set me up for a year! Remember, the Universe hates a vacuum, and we need to have faith through the discomfort.

Here's a few techniques for managing fear:

- *Remember it's only in your mind and push the thoughts away.*
- *If you need to, allow yourself 15 minutes a day to worry and obsess and then stop.*
- *Write a list of all the horrible things that might happen and then engage your rational, logical mind – how likely are these things to happen? Give it a rating scale if you like.*
- *Or you can use my favourite: recognise you're afraid, ask yourself if anyone including you is going to die if you do the thing you're afraid of, and do it anyway!*

Letting Go of Control

Making a change in your life, finding peace, happiness and/or success requires letting go of control, and one of the biggest things I learned – and am still learning and practising – is letting go and trusting in the Universe. Here is this omnipotent, omnipresent thing that has provided many miracles in my life over the years and yet, even now, I still find myself questioning its wisdom! Who am I to know what is right or possible in this world? I am one person with only one view of the world and what is possible. The Universe is all knowing and all seeing.

I believe there is a grand plan for each of us. I believe that when we are restless or unhappy with our lives, it's a sign that we have veered off course. Yes, some people live their entire lives "off course", but if you are in tune with your body, your mind, and your emotions, you know when you're veering off the course. For me, it shows up in both physical and emotional ways: I start slipping into a depression. I can't get out of bed in the morning, I ache everywhere, my back hurts, I get frequent headaches and colds, and I'm bored and restless – never a good combination with me – and nothing seems to excite me anymore. This is my sign, this is how I know that I am off the path and it's time to change. The problem for me often is, change to what? This is where it gets difficult.

It's difficult because we engage our logical minds, we look around for something that we think is the right thing and "ticks all the boxes": it pays enough money, it's close to home, it has benefits, etc., etc., but we never ask ourselves if we'd be happy. We force our ideas of what we should be doing, of the next step onto our life and then, when it goes wrong, we wonder why. The Universe has a plan. You have to watch for the signs and you have to let go of control. Control is just an illusion anyway. Life happens in spite of you, not because of you!

The number of people I see on a regular basis who are miserable at work is astounding… and yet they won't leave, they won't quit. Why? To put it in their words: "I can't quit, I have a family to support". Well, you CAN quit, there are no chains holding you to the chair or your desk. Even when I see people who have worked in government or union jobs and are so miserable that it rubs off on everyone – including their families – they say they "can't" quit. YES, they can!!! They just don't want to!!!

At what cost are you staying stuck in the circumstances of your life? I've told you what happens to me when I'm off the course, when I'm not happy – it shows up in both physical and emotional ways. I don't think I'm alone. I believe many people are like me and walking around with a low-grade depression – they just don't know it. And I don't know about you, but my goal in this life is to live up to my full potential because that's what's going to bring me the most happiness and success. So again, I ask you – you're unhappy in your job? In your relationship? In the place you live? Why don't you change it? Why don't you do something about it? Because likely, you're afraid.

Here's the letting go part: we must try our best. That's all anyone can ask. We show up, do our best and let the Universe take care of the rest. We can't control outcomes, we can't control the future... we have to let go and trust. When we try to control outcomes, we are interfering with the Divine and infinite intelligence of the Universe. So let go. And by the way... worry doesn't do anything. It doesn't help. Somehow we think that if we worry about something, it will prevent it from happening or make things better. It doesn't. Worry doesn't do anything except waste our energy, make us ill, and invite negativity into our lives. So stop worrying and do your best.

Try it today, think of something you would really like to change or something you really want, find somewhere quiet to sit and relax, think about what it is you want – set your intention and ask the Universe for "this or something better". Then let go. See what happens.

The Law of Attraction – Scarcity vs. Abundance

The Law of Attraction works! But not without the Law of Alignment. That is the entire point of this book – to get out of your own way, to escape the invisible prison of your own making.

If you are following the process and beginning to see where you are not in alignment with who you truly are, where your thought processes and beliefs have kept you stuck, then you are moving closer to your centre. This place of centeredness, of balance, of being at one with oneself is the place where the Law of Attraction occurs with little or no effort from us.

The Law of Attraction simply says that like attracts like. That whatever you put out there is what you will get back. That we will attract those people, places and things that match with our vibration. It's back to that radio antenna analogy... we are always sending and receiving energy so the Law of Attraction means that if we place our energy, our focus, on what we wish to attract and it is in keeping with who we are and our purpose, then the Universe will respond.

It sounds simple and in some ways, it is. But there is also "fine print" that we need to be aware of because we can also attract what we *don't* want by placing too much energy and attention on that! So once again it requires that we monitor our thoughts... that we stay positive, that we stay in abundance.

Whatever you place your attention on will grow. It's that simple. So... if we place our attention on the things we *don't* want, the things we are *afraid* of, then they will grow. Changing our view to a positive one, to an abundant one, to a view which focuses on what we do want will attract that. This is the importance of staying in abundance versus scarcity. When we are in scarcity and focusing on not having enough then we stop the flow.

We hold on to things so tightly because we are afraid of losing them that nothing else can get in. Energy is a flow... money is a flow... love is a flow... it comes in and out, and believing that we don't have enough time, energy, money, love, friends or anything else stops the flow. Try focusing on what you do have, how much love, time, energy, money, friends that you do have, practice gratitude for the abundance you have already been blessed with. This is the way to attract more and more positive things into your life.

I know this isn't easy. I think about myself growing up in a household of "scarcity". Two parents who grew up in the UK during the Second World War where food was rationed and there was not enough to go around had created a mindset within them of "there will never be enough" and this got passed on to my sister and me. And, as such, I can fall into that trap very easily... there won't be enough money to pay the bills, there is not enough work next year... I can easily go to the negative place. But if

I really stop to think about it, if I analyse it, I always have enough. I have always had enough and there is no proof that I won't have enough in the future. Quite the opposite. But that doesn't stop my human brain from engaging in old thinking habits from time to time.

We get so stuck on the past and what's happened and we get so caught up in worrying about the future that sometimes we overlook the present. We fail to show gratitude for the things that we already have in our lives. Here's the thing: when we are constantly lusting after things that we don't have, when we believe we "will be happy when... (fill in the blank here) happens" we will in fact never be happy. We are making our happiness conditional on things outside of ourselves and that never brings happiness, only more unhappiness when things don't happen as we expect them to.

To attract what you want you have to be in alignment, you *must* believe you deserve what it is you are trying to attract, and you must focus on what you want not what you don't want. Neither of these is particularly easy so let's practice:

- *Set your intention. What are you wanting to manifest? (Make sure to phrase it positively).*
- *Spend some time visualising it – what does it look like? Visualise it in as much detail as you can.*
- *Then place your attention on achieving it... it will come.*
- *Identify one or two things you can do every day to move closer to your goal? (They don't have to be big things, just something.)*

Priorities

In closing this chapter, it's worth mentioning the issue of priorities. I get caught in this all the time... I think a lot of us do. In my case, I say that my emotional health is always my Number One priority, and I know how to look after that. For me, it means making sure I'm challenged, that I'm not falling back into old thinking patterns, that I'm engaging in activities and surrounding myself with people who make me feel good, not bad. And yet I find myself still getting caught in the trap of my invisible prison... I'm comfortable. I know what to expect. It is time for a change for me, it's time for the next step, and I am taking it and it's really uncomfortable.

I don't like the fact that I have allowed myself to fall into a trap that I am so aware of. I say I want to write a book, do workshops to help people (because escaping your invisible prison is easier and quicker to do in a group setting and it really can change your life in one workshop), offer programs that people can do in the privacy of their own home and speak at conferences instead of doing my usual designing and facilitating workshops for corporate giants. This is what I say... but what do I do? What actions am I taking? I end up focusing my time, efforts, energies and thoughts on something that no longer makes me happy, that I don't want to do anymore, instead of spending time and energy on the things that I do want to do. And if that's the case, aren't I compromising everything I say is Number One on my list? Sigh! I tell you this so you know you are not alone. This is a journey, not a destination, and even after all these years I have again and again been caught in the trap.

As I write this, my actions are not in alignment with what is important to me. If my emotional well-being is so important, why am I not spending time on that? To be fair, I am spending time in meditation each day and reading for continued personal growth, but it's a small amount of time compared to the hours I spend working on corporate training, all the while complaining that I don't want to do this anymore. This is not the way to help change come about. I must align my actions with my priorities. I must spend time on what's important to me because **whatever we focus our attention on grows.**

I learned this from Deepak Chopra, and because I consciously practise this, I know it's true. It looks like this time I have been unconsciously practising it by focusing on the wrong thing – the habit, the old career that it's time to move on from, the thing that pays the bills, the safe thing. I've been focusing on the safe thing. Anyone identify with this?

This is one of the biggest ways we block our ability to manifest. We say something is important and yet, consciously or not, we focus our attention on the things that are less important to us. Whatever we place our attention on grows. So, what are you placing your attention on?

How much of your mind space is taken up with worry about things you can't control?

How much of your energy do you expend complaining and being miserable about conditions and situations that you can change? And don't go to that place that says: "I can't quit my job because….", or "I can't leave my relationship because…", or "I can't lose weight because…", or anything else you tell yourself you can't do! These are excuses! Our minds have an uncanny ability to rationalise anything!

If you stop and look at your day, what are you spending your time on? Does that match with what you say is important to you?

These are powerful considerations.

Other Blocks to Manifesting

Sometimes, try as you might, you just can't break free of patterns in your life. That's because they are not all necessarily from this lifetime. I know two big blocks that have held and continue to hold me back that are not from this lifetime. I may be about to lose some of you here but go and look on YouTube. You can't ignore the evidence of reincarnation. How else do you explain an elephant which can draw a picture of himself or all the children who seem to know things they can't possibly know?

Research a little, and then decide. I do believe in reincarnation and I know I have had many, many lives. I am currently incarnated with other souls whom I have strong connections with because we have incarnated together before. Have you ever had the experience of meeting someone and feeling that you have known them forever? Or had such a deep connection with someone that you can't explain it? These are likely souls whom you have had other incarnations with.

Whether you believe in reincarnation or not, the Universe is omnipotent. We are the Universe and the Universe is us and it has created a magnificent vessel in which a soul can reside. The miracle of your body is truly amazing! And the miracle of your soul is equally amazing. We are the Divine, the Universe incarnated into a physical body to experience itself. We are mind, body and soul, and so to focus on only mind and body would be leaving out a very important component in your health and well-being because sometimes the soul needs some healing and realignment as well.

And as the saying goes, we continue to repeat the same lessons lifetime after lifetime until we learn them, so perhaps what you are struggling with in this lifetime is a lesson you need to learn. It's a test. Your challenge in this life is to break the pattern or patterns that have held you back in past lives and choose what is in your highest good. Choose not to give up your life for others, or stay in relationships too long, or learn to love and value yourself.

Some of us have great gifts that we hide. Why? Why would we hide these great gifts? Maybe we were persecuted in a past life for these very gifts. I know a woman who refuses to go to London (UK). She says when she is there she has a horrible feeling of being strangled. I'd say it's quite likely she had a very bad experience in a past life in London. Possibly involving a noose or an executioner. The Universe is truly a phenomenal place.

Or perhaps a situation in a past life has left such an imprint, a scar if you will, on your soul that it stays with you in future incarnations. Many of us have these. Tears, or scars in the fabric of our soul, in our energy field. The best way I can describe this is to use my own example: for my entire life, I have suffered with low self-esteem; this is no secret. And I've worked hard to build that up and have been very successful with that, but even then, I had this… *thing* that wouldn't go away. We even gave it a name. We called it "the deserving factor".

I was constantly nagged by this feeling that I didn't deserve the good things that were happening to me. Even though I had worked hard to turn my life around and certainly did deserve them, there was something inside me that said: "You don't deserve this". I couldn't figure it out, but it was so bad that when my husband and I had bought our first house, I stopped at one of those Big Box Stores America is famous for and had a melt-down in the Tupperware aisle! I was sobbing uncontrollably, shaking and crying so hard I couldn't breathe. I was buying Tupperware! I knew I wasn't reacting appropriately but I didn't know why. As I drove up to my new home it hit me – my meltdown was "the deserving factor". Somewhere inside of me I did not believe I deserved a new home. No idea where this came from. I had spent over six years by this time re-wiring and re-programming my brain. Of course I deserved this new house, I had worked hard for it. But somewhere inside of me was this "you don't deserve..." thing.

Fast forward a few years to meeting my first spiritual teacher. On our second coaching call one of the first things she said to me was: "I know this will sound strange, but go with me on this... close your eyes..." and she took me through a process where I recalled a past life. I was a very young servant girl living in Smithfield in London around 600 years ago. I lived in a small room and served a wealthy family. The head of the family (the man) raped me and I got pregnant. In my "vision" if that's what you call it, I could see myself sitting on my bed in this very small room at the bottom of this house. The baby had been still born and there was a man from the church next door standing in the corner of the room dressed in a purple robe saying: "The baby died because you don't deserve it! You don't deserve to have a child you dirty little..." I understood immediately where this "deserving factor" had come from. Not from this lifetime but another one, and it left such a huge scar on my soul that it continued to be present in my energy field in this incarnation.

Once I understood where this came from, I could, and did, heal it. You can heal the scars from past lives so they don't interfere with this one.

Sometimes, what keeps us stuck in our invisible prisons (in my circle, in the people attracted to work with me this is quite common) is "programmed" memory and vows from lifetimes ago. This is generally from a religious order or cult of some kind where there is an initiation ceremony and vows are taken.

There are a lot of reincarnated souls suffering in this lifetime from vows of chastity, poverty and obedience that were made many lifetimes ago. It's amazing... it does not matter what this woman does, how hard she works, or how much money she makes, she never has enough. She's always just scraping by. As soon as she gets money, something happens that causes her to have to give it away – her car breaks down, she needs a new computer, she has an unexpected tax bill... it's always something. It doesn't make sense, does it? It's an old vow of poverty, and until it's cleared this woman will continue to have trouble manifesting and keeping things.

As you have been reading this chapter, are you recognising things operating in you that may not be from this lifetime? Programming you can't explain?

My point is that not everything is of this world. It really is mind, body and SOUL. Sometimes what holds us back are things from previous incarnations and to move forward we have to clear those. And yes, there are healing modalities which can do this. You can look in the Resources section for more information about these.

As Your Life Continues

"Believe in yourself! Have faith in your abilities! Without a humble but reasonable confidence in your own powers you cannot be successful or happy."
Norman Vincent Peale

"There are people who make things happen, there are people who watch things happen, and there are people who wonder what happened. To be successful you need to be a person who makes things happen."
Jim Lovell

"If I could give you one gift I would give you the ability to see you as I see you, so you can see how special you truly are."
Unknown

I love the last quote as this is my wish for you. I wish for you to believe, and to see that you are a divine being in human form, deserving of everything this life has to offer.

There are 9 Secrets in this book for a reason. The number '9' is auspicious in Spirituality. It signifies many things including faith, love, spiritual enlightenment and awakening, destiny and soul purpose, inner-wisdom, self-love and freedom. Freedom from the invisible prison of your own creation. You were born a divine being, a divine light. My wish for you is that you uncover your light and shine it as brightly as possible to show others the way.

I've shared with you my journey, how I have learned to see our human condition and what drives our behaviours – from the emotional part of our brain, not the rational part of it. I've shared my understanding of the science of Quantum Physics as it relates to the practice of Spirituality as a way of helping you understand that we are all just a big radio antenna… always emitting and receiving waves of energy.

I've used myself as a case-study to illustrate some of the struggles I have faced and how I worked through them, and given some examples of issues my clients have had and have worked through. My hope is that if some of these situations resonate for you, you now know that you are not alone, and that there is a way you can make things better for yourself.

At this point I would love to tell you that things will all work out perfectly… they will, but in the way they are supposed to, which is not necessarily the way you wish them to. Even after all the studying and work I've done, my life has not been perfect. There have been many life-altering challenges that have been thrown at me over the years, and you know what? I've been OK. I live the principles I have set out in this book, and because of that, while I've had to endure some tough times, I have *always* been OK. I have always made it through to the other side more confident and resilient than before. And you can too.

You've got this! I know you can do it because I have done it and my clients have done it – now you can too. But you do have to work at it! Remember it's a journey not a destination and that some days you will have more success than others – and that's OK! Be kind to yourself!

So to finish – my challenge to you is… what will you do for yourself and when will you do it? You have choice, there is always choice – what will you choose?'

> *"Every time you look outside of yourself for approval,*
> *or happiness or self-esteem you are disempowering*
> *yourself. We have choices! Make your choice! It's*
> *your life, your happiness, your time, your self-respect*
> *(which is why it's called **self**-respect). You choose."*
> **Susan Armstrong**

Additional Resources

If you've read the entire book – *congratulations!* It's a great start, particularly if you are doing the exercises contained in this book.

For more information, you can go to:

My blog: **www.whateveryouputoutthere.com**

My website: **www.escapeyourinvisibleprison.com**

If you just need a weekly pick me up, then please sign up for my blog as it's a great place to start.

If you're not ready for group work just yet, then please go to the website where you can download more in-depth programs to work through at your own pace in the comfort of your own home.

Of course, doing the work yourself can be harder than doing it in a group, so if you're ready, I would always recommend a workshop (and it doesn't have to be mine!). There is something very powerful about doing this work together.

If you are serious about escaping the invisible prison you keep yourself locked in, if it's time for you, you can find a schedule and outline of workshops listed on my website **www.escapeyourinvisibleprison.com**

Here's one of my favourite workshops:

Escape Your Invisible Prison!

Overcome the barriers to your personal and professional success, happiness and freedom!

Are you finally ready to break free of what holds you back and create the successful, fulfilling, happy life you desire? Join us for this unique and deeply healing workshop:

- *Are you feeling stuck?*
- *Are you frustrated because you can't seem to move forward?*
- *Do you want to break free of your self-limiting beliefs and uncover who you TRULY are?*
- *Do you want to develop your confidence and self-esteem and find your voice?*
- *Do you finally want to have peace and happiness in your life?*

Then join me for this unique workshop combining emotional healing with Soul-Realignment™ work. In this workshop, you will be able to re-wire your thought processes as well as discover your unique soul profile and energy centres. The combination of removing the emotional and psychological blocks to happiness and success with the realignment of the soul and clearing of any negative energies and blockages allows you to experience the freedom of being who you truly are at a deep soul level.

Here's wishing you a successful, peaceful and happy future!

About the Author

"Abuse, street gangs, motorcycle gangs and being shot... No, it is not the character progression and plot synopsis of the next Bruce Willis or Jet Li action blockbuster, but rather a summary of the struggles and experiences through which Susan Armstrong actually lived! Most people outside of a movie set would not survive any one of these wrecking balls, let alone all five. But Susan Armstrong not only survived them, she went on to reinvent herself, establish her own company, author a book and use her personal experiences as the blueprint for helping others to be successful and achieve their greatest potential."

Christopher Cussat,
Recovery Solutions Magazine, July 2006

SUSAN ARMSTRONG is a gifted personal growth teacher, author and international speaker and workshop leader, working with people to help them overcome their barriers to personal and professional success. For the past 20 years, Susan has worked with global organisations to help them improve the way they do business. Whether working with corporations or at personal growth seminars, Susan is able to captivate and motivate her audience with her warm style and entertaining wit.

Susan practises what she preaches as she herself has learned to overcome a great deal of faulty thinking as chronicled in the book ***An Invisible Prison, a true story of survival***. A bright child, destined to accomplish great things, she was lacking two very important components of success: coping skills and a sense of self. As a result of these deficiencies, instead of doing well in school and going on to a rewarding career, she chose an alternate route. Susan has spent many years developing her own sense of esteem and accomplishment, and now shares her knowledge and experience with others so they might find their own happiness and success.

Susan Armstrong has been honoured by the Canadian Association for Mental Health as an "Extraordinary Person", and she appears on many television and radio shows including Discovery Channel's *Health on the Line*, Life Television, CHTV *Morning Live*, Rogers TV's *Woman to Woman*, One-on-One, and is a repeat guest on the Valder Beebe Show, an award-winning spiritual talk show.

www.escapeyourinvisibleprison.com

Lightning Source UK Ltd.
Milton Keynes UK
UKOW05f2320240217
295305UK00010B/102/P